THE SANDSTONE PAPERS

ON THE CRISIS OF
CONTEMPORARY LIFE

Marty Glass

THE
SANDSTONE
PAPERS

*ON THE CRISIS OF
CONTEMPORARY LIFE*

Second
Edition

SOPHIA PERENNIS

HILLSDALE NY

Second, revised edition 2005
First edition, Threshold Books 1986

Series editor: James R. Wetmore

For information, address:
Sophia Perennis, P.O. Box 611
Hillsdale NY 125295
sophiaperennis.com

Library of Congress Cataloging-in-Publication Data

Glass, Marty, 1938–
Sandstone papers : on the crisis of contemporary life /
Marty Glass.—2nd ed.

p. cm.
Includes bibliographical references.
ISBN 1 59731 048 4 (pbk: alk. paper)
1. Civilization, Modern—950– 2. Conduct of life.
3. Spiritual life. I. Title.
CB430.G57 2005
909.8301—dc22   2005031312

CONTENTS

Preface
Second Edition

I'm writing this Preface in May 2005. *The Sandstone Papers*, subtitled "On the Crisis of Contemporary Life," was written in the early 1980s, twenty years ago. The human race has been feverishly busy, as usual, making history, and with constantly accelerating velocity. My task has been to review the text for relevance to our current situations, to determine if it can claim to be anything more than an account of how things appeared to and concerned thoughtful people back then. Twenty years might be a long time ago or only yesterday. The same issues may be reappearing in different forms; our lives may express the unfolding of themes and trends visible not only in the '80s of this century but visible to prescient people decades or even centuries ago. It would seem unlikely that we wage our convictions, wars, and social tensions in a whole new ball game.

The format of the book determines our approach. *The Sandstone Papers* presents a fictional conference addressing the perceived crises of the period. A fictional editor, John Street (my address at the time in Oakland), has been invited to attend the conference and select for subsequent publication six papers from among the twenty delivered. The "authors" of these papers were, of course, also fictional—my "alter-egos," as Huston Smith defines them in his back-cover endorsement. We can begin to address the question of relevance by reviewing Street's catalog of "crises" as he lists them in his Introduction.

He begins with what seemed overwhelmingly self-evident to him as it was to everyone in those anxious years: "the nuclear peril." Still relevant? Certainly not in the same form.

But since what was called then "the balance of terror" has now been replaced, in the wake of 9/11—the single most consequential and politically exploited event in the intervening years—by "The Age of Terror," as President Bush defined the situation, it could be argued, and has been, that a "nuclear peril," with its concordant atmosphere of fear, has assumed a new and more insidious guise. As for the rest of the specific concrete crises catalogued by Street, it appears that, other than the locales of conventional warfare and the issues over which they are engaged, little has changed. His analysis becomes more interesting to us today when he refers to "the more subtle, but perhaps more fundamental crisis" of "dehumanization." Deep stuff here! Something more people think about, perhaps, than speak about. He sees a confrontation, in the mind of society and in the societal issues the confrontation generates, between "scientists" and "humanists." Certainly this insight rings a bell in the musings of keen observers. Technology is the reigning and but feebly contested power in all areas of our lives. On the whole, the world Street sees is very familiar to us. Trends and themes have, it seems to me, unfolded and assumed new forms, and this very fact of implacable impersonal one-directional unfolding, one might claim, one might feel, unveils an ominous jagged edge beneath the surface of events that many people experience, I believe, in the privacy of haunting presentiment. It's enthroned Technology, Lewis Mumford's "Myth of the Machine." Street saw it coming; but, in his conventional decency and growing detachment, he didn't fully feel it, didn't manage to take its full measure.

Briefly, the six speakers. Walter Frank's paper, a description of the unchanging "big picture" in our lives, is the most general, the most encompassing, and the most distant, in its way, from "current events," and, given its metaphysical distance from historical affairs, has lost nothing of its relevance. Amy Rosenblatt's "spiritual psychology" is timeless and should strike a chord with the many people engaged now

upon spiritual paths. Mark Harrison was the only marxist at
the conference. Street described him as "a marxist in his diagnosis and a humanist in his prescription." There are many
such today, not perhaps in this country but certainly in
Europe. Post-modernist "critical thinkers" appeal with conviction and near unanimity to the mature Marx of *Capital I*
and the *Gründrisse* in their analyses of our plight. Harrison
was one of the university activists of the times, familiar to
those of us old enough to remember the Vietnam Era. Louis
di Prima's paper, in its fierce concentration on the nuclear
war issue, is the one most likely to have lost its punch. But if
we disengage the nuclear aspect and look to its evocation of
the "end times," we will certainly be recalled to the point of
view proclaimed in certain "fundamentalist Christian" quarters today. Same theme, new guise. Sister Angela's mystical
rhapsodies are for all time, perhaps with a vengeance now.
She saw more than Street. She was beyond him. Finally,
Pierre Flynn, my favorite, the shrewd and only humorist
among the participants. Street explains, in his Introduction to
Flynn's paper, why he placed it last in the book. And, I might
add, Street finally emerges, in the phrase I borrow from
Henry James' description of Lambert Strether in *The Ambas-
sadors*, as "the fine central intelligence" of *The Sandstone
Papers*. We see this clearly in the fragments of the journal he
kept at the conference and in his Epilog. There's something
of him in all of us.

The book carries a Bibliography, and there have been many
very fine texts I would add were I to write such a book today,
as well as many fine texts I was unaware of at the time of
writing. For a redefinition of the "confrontation" Street saw
at Sandstone, I might mention Benjamin Barber's brilliant
Jihad vs. McWorld. And the post-modernist archive is bristling
with keen insights into our urgencies. I might say, perhaps by
way of apology and compensation for the shortcomings of
the present text, that my own *YUGA: An Anatomy of our Fate*
pursues with hopefully deeper penetration, and this time a

consistency, the themes presented at Sandstone twenty years ago.

One thing, however, is clear, and must be emphasized. One thing hasn't changed at all, hasn't become irrelevant or outdated, and is truer now than ever, as it has always been true. Street concludes his Introduction by pointing out that the six speakers "all take for granted that the roots of things, like the answers to our more compelling questions, lie deep." He refers to "their stubborn fidelity to this postulate of depth," and insists that "they are all, with individual emphases and whether or not they are formally affiliated with a particular confession, profoundly religious people." In these times, more than ever before, we can be quite certain that only those public witnesses whose message emerges from that stubborn faithful postulate can illuminate our troubled lives, our constellation of crises, our ineffaceable promise. And it is not only Truth that resides in depth, but Bliss as well. Where we find one, we find the other.

THE SANDSTONE PAPERS
On the Crisis of Contemporary Life

A Conference
held at
The Adam Bell Center
of the
College of the West
in
Sandstone, California

Sponsored by the Hardwood Fund Foundation

Papers Edited By
John Street

To the memory of
Sister Angela Maria Prescott
1899-1987

On behalf of the Board of Directors of the Hardwood Fund, I would like to thank the American scholars who were kind enough to take time off from their busy schedules to participate in the Sandstone Conference. We hope that the publication of these papers will contribute toward a greater and wider understanding of the roots of the present crisis, and that from this understanding the courage and wisdom to alter our present ominous course will emerge. I would also like to thank Mr. John Street for his able editing of the papers and for his willingness to share his perceptive reactions to the Conference.

Peter Morrisey
Eureka, California

Introduction

When Peter Morrisey, Secretary-Treasurer of the Board of Directors of the Hardwood Fund, asked me if I would be willing to attend the Sandstone Conference and edit the papers presented there for subsequent publication by the Fund, my first question was "Why me?" He explained that the Board, given the universal concern which the Conference seeks to inform, was aiming at a larger audience for this publication than academia and wanted an editor qualified to serve as a bridge between the island of university scholarship and the mainland of America's educated readers. As a non-specialist with an editorial career in public education, I would be asked to select those papers which, in their style, content and approach, most addressed the needs and encouraged the interest of a readership wider than the community of scholars from which the the participants were invited. I would be given free rein to select six from among the twenty papers to be presented, and my comments, on the papers, the participants and the Conference as a whole, would be subject only to space limitations and, of course, final approval by the Board. After a few days of reflection I accepted Mr. Morrisey's offer.

In this period of reflection, and during the month of June, I adjusted my editoral agenda for July, which as it turned out was fairly routine, and devoted some time to examining my own perspective on "the crisis of contemporary life." What was its content?

The nuclear peril, of course, in the forms of weaponry, power plant accidents and disposal of radioactive wastes, came to mind first, followed in grim procession by the dilemma of environmental degradation and the exhaustion of planetary resources, the pressures of overpopulation both upon those dwindling resources and upon governmental

1

stability, widespread judicial brutality and blatant violations
of human rights, the pollution, both physical and spiritual, of
urban life, the continuous outbreaks of small-scale "conventional" warfare, especially in the mideast and Central America, and the economic crisis in all its aspects: recession, infla-
tion, unemployment, business failure and the drastic
cutbacks in social services due to mounting budgetary con-
straints. This list seemed more than sufficient to warrant
alarm.

I also attempted to refine my view of the more subtle, but
perhaps more fundamental, crisis referred to by certain
thinkers, generally disaffected with the modern world, as the
crisis of "dehumanization." In this interpretation, mechanism
in all its forms—as actual machinery, as impersonal bureaucracy, as pure technique—is enslaving, if not actually replac-
ing, humanity: in modern industrialized mass societies, we
are told, people have lost touch with their earthly identity as
well as their history, and are rapidly becoming the passive
creatures of technology, as viewers of TV, as motorists, as
slaves to home appliances, and as workers manipulated and
diminished by the devices of scientific management. The
books of Lewis Mumford, and other modern philosophers
less well known, revolve about this collapse of the humanist
tradition as a guiding force in society, and, I must confess, at
the time of my acceptance of the Board's assignment I had
become persuaded that the "dehumanization" argument was
at least as cogent as those which focussed solely upon the
improvement of material conditions and upon the level of
reality accessible to statistical definition. The reasoned analyses contained in Mumford's *The Myth of the Machine*, in
Jacques Ellul's *The Technological Society*, in Herbert Marcuse's
One Dimensional Man and in Siegfried Giedion's *Mechanization
Takes Command*, four classic critiques of modern technology,
ought certainly to be represented at the Conference.

Finally, I reviewed what might be called the ideological
perspectives likely to clamor for a hearing at Sandstone.

Modern theologians perceive the crisis in religious terms and deplore a decline in faith; psychologists perceive a crisis in social and sexual identity as traditional roles crumble under the double impact of liberation movements and economic recession; ecologists bewail the spoilation and poisoning of the planet; socialists condemn capitalism and capitalists condemn socialism; communists identify imperialism as the devil and imperialists identify communism as the Anti-Christ; women indict the patriarchy and the patriarchy wrings its hands over the flight from traditional values; labor denounces the greed of management and management denounces the greed of labor; the United States defends itself against the aggressive expansionism of the Soviet Union, and vice versa. And so on. It became obvious to me that the infrastructure, as it were, of the crisis of contemporary life must consist of competing interpretations of that very crisis, interpretations, furthermore, representing interest groups whose competition is far more than verbal.

I arrived in Sandstone, amid a bustle of other arrivals, on June 30th. There were to be twenty participants and about fifty auditors at the Conference. According to the brief biographies kindly supplied to me by Dr. Warren Holleman, Chancellor of the College of the West, all the participants had higher degrees, several of them in more than one field, except Mr. di Prima, a brilliant and serious writer associated by the rather superficial conventions of literary criticism with the off-campus intelligentsia who used to be called "beat." All the participants were Americans and all, again with the exception of Mr. di Prima, had lectured widely both here and abroad and were highly regarded for their professional competence.

The Conference ran for two weeks with papers presented each morning and afternoon. A few participants arrived and left the same day, many stayed longer, some stayed the entire two weeks. After each paper was delivered there was an informal discussion among the participants present; auditors were welcome to contribute. The atmosphere was generally friendly and lively, occasionally solemn, never acerbic and always courteous. The two basic camps into which the Conference spontaneously divided itself, which might be called the "humanists" and the "technocrats," managed to find each other amusing rather than menacing or absurd and occasionally even interesting, although perhaps more as individuals than as scholars. There was genuine mutual respect, amounting at times, at least so it appeared to me, to compassion. Many of them knew each other already.

The papers I finally selected, as you will see, are distinguished as much by their literary merit as by their depth of content—except, perhaps, for Walter Frank's, a paper of great depth and significance which I included despite its competent but unexceptional prose style because in its impartiality and broadness of scope it seemed to serve as a background to the entire Conference, and because, like the other five, it was not encumbered with footnotes or a scientific vocabulary. The other five, as I have suggested, are all outstanding, in my judgment, for their literary style as well as their philosophical substance. With the exception of Mr. di Prima's contribution, whose colloquial style reinforces rather than detracts from its powerful sincerity and chilling finality, I regard these papers as "demanding but readable," the phrase that came to my mind while I was narrowing down my choices to the six I finally settled upon—which are printed here, not accidentally but significantly, in the order in which I heard them.

Why "significantly"?

I had not expected, when I accepted Mr. Morrisey's generous offer, that my experience at the Conference would entail the stress of personal drama. I had understood myself to be carrying out a specific assignment, an extension of my daily work, which I have always carefully, and I believe prudently, isolated from my private life. This was not to be the case. As it turned out, the questions proposed by these six papers determined the stages of a psychological—I hesitate to say spiritual—drama which led me to reexamine the meaning of

my own life, at least in certain of its aspects, and to acknowledge the concrete and sobering reality of my own "destiny,"
a term which I had hitherto regarded as theatrical or
metaphysical.

As a result of this unexpected privilege—such experiences
being rightfully perceived as privileges—there are two separate but overlapping dimensions to my experience at the Conference, and to my editorial commentary, which I will call the
formal dimension and the personal dimension. The formal
dimension takes precedence since this book is, after all, a
selection from papers delivered at the Sandstone Conference
on the crisis of contemporary life, not an autobiographical
fragment describing a crisis in the editor's private life, but it
was the joint decision of Mr. Morrisey and myself that the
personal dimension of my experience at the Conference
should also be included in this volume because, far from
jarring with the conception of the book, it demonstrates the
relevance of university scholarship, at least in one individual's life, to the larger world outside the academy, this demon-
stration of relevance, as fortunate as it was inadvertent,
being precisely the goal the Board hoped to achieve by the
engagement of my editorial responsibility. Our decision
being made, there remained only questions of discretion and
format. Since I kept a journal during the Conference, in
which the habitual reserve my colleagues find so entertain-
ing was somewhat relaxed, both questions were happily
resolved with the plan of including excerpts from this journal, from which the more personal material, of course, would
be deleted, in my introductory remarks about the six speakers and their papers.

There is, then, a dual format to this book, in that the
Conference, or six papers from it, is presented both in its
formal dimension, as a public event whose significance
resides in the light it may cast upon the present crisis, and, in
its personal dimension, as the occasion for a private drama of
reassessment in which that same crisis, illuminated by the

papers delivered, takes possession of an individual's life and reveals it to be a microcosm of the globlal reality. The focus, however, is always upon the papers themselves.

With regard now to the formal dimension, I would like to state without further ado the criterion upon which I based my selection. That criterion was *impracticality*. The perhaps startling characteristic by which I distinquished the six papers I chose from the fourteen I rejected was that these six offer no practical solution whatsoever to the crisis of contemporary life. The other fourteen papers all, in varying degrees and within various fields of scientific specialization, dealt with geopolitical and technological analyses and proposals, often buttressed by charts, graphs and statistics; many of them couldn't have been written without the assistance of modern computer technology. Some scenarios seemed to me decidedly utopian, or at least improbable, while other papers were sufficiently technical, I am tempted to say numerical, as to render the role of human beings ambiguous if not invisible. All assumed that the crisis was due to faulty financial, political or technological structural models and could be remedied by alternative organizational forms.

I justify my admittedly impertinent exclusion of practical approaches to the contemporary crisis on the sole ground that we have all heard them many times before: indeed, they are *all* that we ever hear, and to my mind they are beginning to sound almost sinister in their tedious obeisance before the mystique of technology and the gimmickry of systems, as if their true intent is to lull us into a false sense of security or to convince us that only "experts" can understand our world and make the correct decisions. There is in this country, I believe, a submerged consensus, expressing itself usually in the mode of irony, that to the degree that technical methods have been implemented, whether in the realm of public education, governmental budgeting, global politics, managerial strategies or environmental "engineering," they almost invariably create more, and deeper, problems than they solve. I

feel that it is time we lend a sympathetic ear to those perspectives which are less practical in a technical sense, less
bewitched by expedience, but perhaps more practical in a
profounder sense, in that they go to the roots of the problem,
which are, I would argue, in the human person, in humanity's
historical and cosmic situations, and in the values, life-
oriented or death-oriented, which materialize into societies
and civilizations. In such perspectives human beings are not
seen as interchangeable components who merely need to be
inserted into the appropriate geopolitical or technological
grid, but rather as thoroughly miraculous multi-dimensional
beings who, despite the most arduous efforts, have never
been able fully to implement their valid conclusions about
how they ought to behave or to establish their happiness on
ground much firmer than the quicksand beneath our feet
today: beings, in a word, whose dismal failure to foresee the
consequences of their evolutionary creativity condemns
them to perpetually reexamine the mystery of their
existence.

The six papers collected here, however, despite the basically non-technical approach they share, are by no means on
that account consistent with one another. They are rather
like six views of the same mountain, that mountain being our
human condition in its permanent and historical plights.
From the desperation of Louis di Prima to the faith of Amy
Rosenblatt, from the ironic realism of Pierre Flynn to the
marxist humanism of Mark William Harrison, and from the
intellectual detachment of Walter Frank to the spiritual dis-
engagement of Sister Angela Prescott, these papers, each in
its own way, aspire to address us in the depth and wholeness
of our present reality, often reaching us with a clarity that
ought not fail to touch a resonating chord in the consciences
of people whose concern and humility are sincere. There are
no answers in this book. There are, instead, a wisdom and
honesty, all too rare in these times, without which we cannot
even ask the right questions. Few would dispute the gloomy

observation that there is little friendship between the wisdom we have acquired, at a cost of such great suffering and sacrifice, and the values and hypotheses which shape the real world in which we all live and work. We face a crisis, I believe, because world leadership is no longer guided, if indeed it ever was, by the saving truths to whose memory, with all that the word implies, the papers collected here are devoted. If there are notes of despair in these texts I think they are intended not to mock our optimism, but rather to urge us to face squarely the consequences of our deeds before it is too late. They are intended, in other words, to awaken us from the complacent cynicism with which we view our own fate.

In the personal dimension, the center of my experience at Sandstone was the realization that I, and the world, are something quite different, and rather more grand, than I had thought we were. It was not a revelation, for I have had my intimations, but rather a confirmation or reassurance. I am simply aware now, thanks to Sandstone, of a demand to look more deeply into myself and into the world than has been my habit. I have no present intention to depart from the path I have been following. But the basis upon which I make decisions has been subtly altered, the principles subtly modified.

The six speakers whose papers you are about to read all take for granted that the roots of things, like the answers to our more compelling questions, lie deep—indeed often buried in that invisible substratum of the visible world, accessible only to intuition and the related "spiritual" faculties, whose existence has been consistently attested by poets and prophets and complacently denied, perhaps at their peril and our own, by our public servants and their advisers. In their stubborn fidelity to this postulate of depth, as in their unabashed recourse and appeal to our intuitive as well as our rational capacities, they are all, with individual emphases and whether or not they are formally affiliated with a particular confession, profoundly religious people.

It is perhaps possible that the human race will save itself. I think our success will be more likely, however, and more easily defined, it we seek to heal ourselves in the spirit of penitance rather than confidence, and of gratitude rather than congratulation.

John Street
San Francisco
September, 1987

Cosmos and History:
The Two Which Are One

Introduction

Walter Frank, the opening speaker at the Conference, received his Ph.D. in Philosophy from Washington University in 1949 and a Ph.D. in Romance Languages from Yale University in 1959. He was born in 1921 in Hartford, Connecticut, was awarded a Purple Heart in World War II, and served on several civil rights commissions in the decade of the sixties. I was told that his colleagues regard him as a radical in his life and a conservative in his thought.

A lanky athletic-looking man, Dr. Frank is almost disarmingly alert; he gave me the impression of someone who spends a considerable amount of his time patiently reasoning with people, a pastime I am not unfamiliar with myself. He delivered his paper with obvious professional ease, speaking conversationally and punctuating major points with voice emphasis and occasional gestures. I chose his essay, as I remarked earlier, because of its great scope. It seems to me, if I may be permitted the play on words, to serve as a perspective on perspectives, and I suspect that Dr. Holleman, who reviewed the papers and arranged the schedule, may have placed it first on the program for that very reason.

I introduce at this point a brief passage from the journal I made reference to in the Introduction. It was written on the evening of the day Dr. Frank presented his paper. The "Helen" referred to is my late wife; I have been a widower for nine years.

> I found his paper comforting. To be able to view the world and one's life in a setting so vast and impersonal, and yet also so beautiful, must eventually engender a durable inner peace. One

feels that everything is perfect as it is, and that one's participation in life, no matter how it may appear to be limited by restrictive circumstances or weaknesses of character, is actually insured by the nature of things to be as full as anyone else's. No one stands on the periphery condemned to the role of a mere spectator enviously watching the real performers. We are all caught up in the great adventure of life. "The two which are one" are within us all. I know Helen would have been exhilarated.

Cosmos and History:
The Two Which Are One

by Walter Frank

The two terms I shall be using in this paper, cosmos and history, point to a distinction known by many other names, each of which illuminates yet another facet of the one fundamental polarity in which all things are immersed.

Here are some of those names: spirit and matter, eternity and time, the sacred and the profane, the changeless and the changing, soul and body, being and becoming, the spiritual and the secular, the cyclical and the linear, essence and existence, the universal and the particular, the one and the many, the meaningful and the meaningless, immortality and death, the celestial and the terrestrial, tradition and invention, archetype and instance, reality and illusion, God and the world. In the language of the Vedanta, the aboriginal revelation of India, Atman and Maya. In the language of the immortal Dharma, known in the West as Buddhism, Nirvana and Samsara. In the symbolism of Islam, the final revelation in this cycle, the Face and the Veil.

In some cases—soul and body, for example—the second term is a covering or container of the first; in other cases—the universal and the particular, for example—the first manifests itself in the second; in all cases the two terms or realms either interpenetrate or imply each other.

The most important thing to know about these polarities, and about life understood in their light, is that the two realms to which they refer are really one. It is neither necessary nor possible to choose between the two dimensions of the Entirety called, in this paper, Cosmos and History. They are the Two which are really One, the warp and woof of the great tapestry upon which all things are woven. What is needed is to

13

penetrate the apparent opposition of the two dimensions, to
reconcile their apparent conflict, in the actual living of life. All
life, in every moment, is the point of intersection of the Holy
Cross, the Eternal Now where the vertical, eternity, inter-
sects with the horizontal, time, where the divine and the
human become one and we are saved. I said the divine and the
human: I could as well have said being and becoming, the
celestial and the terrestrial, God and the world—or cosmos
and history. When we reflect upon the universe the polarities
immediately emerge, because the mind, whose vehicle is
language, separates and analyzes: this is its nature. By the
same token, however, the nature of life is to unify. The two
realms are as inevitably separated in the mind as they are
inescapably unified in the act of living. The unity of cosmos
and history cannot be known or uttered, it can only be lived.
"As is Nirvana, so is Samsara: Do not think there is any
distinctions," we read in *Saraha's Treasury of Songs*.

I mention the actual unity of the two realms here at the
beginning of this paper rather than at the end, which might
seem more logical, for two reasons.

First, the entire following discussion, which is devoted to
explaining and elaborating, rather thoroughly, the cosmos
and history polarity, will read differently if it is is kept in mind
that this polarity is always transcended in life, where the two
are one; the truth of actual unity should be recalled throughout and sought for in every illustration of the distinction
between the two.

Second, there can be no doubt that the cosmos emerges
from this discussion as a happier place than history, and I
wish to respond at the outset to possible protests from those
political activists among my esteemed colleagues who are
engaged in historical struggles and who might be turned
away by a discourse which seems to undermine or disparage
their commitment. Insofar as the two are really one, of
course, there is no issue. But there is a sense in which it is
true, independent of prejudice, that cosmic existence is and

was happier than historic existence.

The Fall in the Garden of Eden was, among many other things, the Fall into Time. The expulsion from Eden marked the transition in humanity's spiritual biography from paradisal timelessness to suffering and death. All revelations are addressed to a fallen humanity, whether the Fall is interpreted as a consequence of Sin, a consequence of Ignorance, a schism between existence and essence, or the inevitable separation of the Manifestation from the Principle. The first of the Four Noble Truths is the truth of suffering. By the same token, of course, all revelations provide a remedy, "the one thing needful."

The reality of historical suffering, however, hardly needs to be confirmed by appeal to revelation. For the vast majority of humankind, the arrival of history—in the form of civilization, the market economy, imperialism and colonialism, the white race or urban life—meant suffering, and the loss of the traditional way of life was lamented. Cosmic existence really offered a happier experience than historical existence, at least in the testimony of those who knew both, just as, after the Fall, the cosmic dimension of life—primarily nature and religion—tends to offer consolation while the historical dimension poses challenges. But none of this should imply— and here I respond to political activists—that historical engagement is pointless or destructive. We are all summoned to bear witness to the truth. We are all summoned to stand in solidarity with efforts to defend or advance human well-being, whether we interpret our solidarity as a commitment to progress, an historical category, or an expression of love, a cosmic category: socialists and Christians, feminists and Buddhists alike demonstrate against nuclear weapons research. Happy or unhappy, history is now our dominant reality: within that reality the intrinsic and noblest virtue is responsibility: the virtues, in turn, are cosmic: again, the Two are really One.

These points being clarified, and with the unity and equal

dignity of cosmos and history now clearly in mind, let us
continue our examination of their distinction.

Human beings, as we have seen, live in the two realms
simultaneously, and each realm defines their situation in its
own way. Someone's historical situation, for example, might
be as follows: John Smith, American citizen, living in San
Francisco, Social Security Number 123-45-6789, employed
with the Bank of America, married, father of two children,
residing at 321 Main Street, travelling the Bayshore Freeway
at 5:45 PM on May 26, 1982. Smith's cosmic situation might
be: immortal soul on its journey to eternity. The first description may refer to Smith as matter, the second to Smith as
spirit, or the first to the apparent Smith and the second to the
actual Smith, or the first to the meaningless in Smith and the
second to the meaningful in Smith.

Another approach to the polarity is to think in terms of
qualities, on the one hand, and facts on the other. Courage
and compassion, for example, are qualities, eternal realities
independent of time and place (the permanent); the War of
the Roses, however, is a fact: it occurred only once at a
definite time and in a definite place (the transitory). The
cosmic point of view emphasizes the reality of qualities, the
historical point of view emphasizes the reality of facts, which
are frequently quantities. From the cosmic point of view all
specific events—the War of the Roses, for example—are
merely occasions for the deployment of cosmic realities: occasions for the individual souls involved to ascend or descend
the hierarchy of being, the ladder of cosmic values—to be
equal or unequal to a spiritulal challenge, to choose rightly or
wrongly, to be noble or vile, to act out of love or out of fear.
Specific events (instance) are seen as interchangeable—a war
is a war, if you've seen one you've seen them all (archetype)—
and therefore meaningless on their own terms: "There is
nothing new under the sun." The objective world is merely
the meaningless and undifferentiated raw material from
which the individual soul creates reality, which is the self-

discovery of spirit. From the historical point of view, on the other hand, the sequence of events is reality itself, it is fraught with significance on its own terms, and the qualities or subjective dimension—courage and compassion, for example—are merely incidental: "the human factor." History emphasizes the outer, cosmos the inner.

History confronts people with a *series* of values and definitions, changing all the time, changing *with* time—yesterday we raised children *that* way: today we raise children *this* way; yesterday we did things *that* way: today we do things *this* way; yesterday we believed *that*: today we believe *this*; yesterday *that* was beautiful: today *this* is beautiful; yesterday we thought *that* was right: today we think *this* is right—and the cosmos confronts them with *one set* of values and definitions, changeless and eternal, woven into the very fabric of existence, constant as the stars: the qualities of things, the virtues and the vices, the stages and episodes of human growth and development, the permanent and essential characteristics of human nature. From the cosmic point of view only the unchanging is *significant*, only the unchanging is *real*, only the unchanging is *true*; from the historical point of view, reality is the continuous unfolding of unique events whose significance derives precisely from their role in the linear sequence itself: reality *is* change: the march of time. In history people are conditioned, confined to and defined by a particular point in the evolution of the human race (becoming, atonement): in the cosmos they break through into a timeless present, unconditioned, an Eternal Now (being, salvation). History is the temporal affairs of humanity, an adventure in time: cosmos is the permanent reality in which people incarnate eternal archetypes and discover eternal truths. A human biography is likely to reflect cosmic realities in childhood and adolescence, historical realities in active adult life, and cosmic realities again in old age, although where the impact of historical oppression, overt or subtle, is particularly intense this pattern will be altered.

Religion, folklore, fairy tales, myths, jokes, maxims and adages refer to an unchanging human nature and appeal to "the eternal verities" (the sacred): they are cosmic. The newspapers and television, on the other hand, reporting the *news* (the profane), the endless waterfall of events, appearing and disappearing in ceaseless succession, bombard people with history. Those who tend to love Nature are partial to the cosmic dimension (the cyclical, the eternal); those who look forward to visiting Washington D.C. or Rome are usually thinking of themselves as historical (the linear, the temporal). Those who think of themselves as identical with their social functions and definitions (the contingent, the body)—their work, their civic and family life, their political affiliation, their nationality, their regional origins—tend to see themselves as historical; those who regard these functions and definitions as external or accidental, as a role they play, and think of their real self (the free, the soul) as the unencumbered witness of their earthly performance, tend toward a cosmic point of view. Those who long for "the good old days" when everything hung together and had its place, who view with poignant or bitter regret the vanishing of the Native American, are nostalgic for the cosmos; those who believe in scientific and political progress, who visit expositions, industrial fairs and museums, who join political organizations and identify with political movements, and who are well-informed about current events are committed to history. Those who see the coming elections, the republican administration, the oil cartels, and a cold war between Communism and Democracy interpret the world historically: those who see ignorance, corruption, violence, fear and greed interpret the world from a cosmic point of view. The first see existence: the second see essence. The first see the particular: the second see the universal.

In general terms the East has been cosmic and the West historical; all "uncivilized" people, of course, were cosmic. History begins with the donation of absolute significance to the passing stream of events by the interventionism of the God of the Old Testament prophets, and with an Incarnation *in time* and by which we *measure* time. Historical events now acquire for the first time a value in themselves because they are determined by the will of God: no longer manifestations of archetypes whose meaning and source transcend the particular occasion, events in the world of the Judaic elites derived their meaning from their location in a one-way time which was a revelation of God's will. This was a religious revolution of quite stupendous consequence. Paradoxically, the decline of religion in the West, meaning the secularization of reality, accompanied the further, and finally complete, invasion of history: once given its start, once the world of archetypal repetitions had been superseded, history took an a life of its own in which "God's will" gradually disappeared— at least for most people. The "histories" of classical antiquity, on the other hand, are really pedagogy; characters and events are commemorated not for their significance in a one-way stream of events but as exemplary models of appropriate or inappropriate behavior: virtue or weakness, good judgment or bad judgment, wisdom or folly. These "histories" serve the same function as myths, or the history plays of Shakespeare. The significance of horizontal reality is still vertical, as in the cosmologies of Hinduism and Buddhism.

In a cosmic setting, as in the archaic and traditional societies, social life perpetuated itself by the mimesis or reenactment (a more precise word, because it's actually a case of the *same thing* happening repeatedly, like laughter or the return of Spring, rather than an imitation) of ancestral ways: people did what had always been done because that was the way to do it, because that was The Way life was exemplary. In historical societies, on the contrary, or civilizations, social life perpetuated itself through the mimesis of innovations, of creative individuals: people began to do things in new ways rather than perpetually repeat the archetypal gestures which annulled the passage of time, they became inventive and imaginative, change became constant and acquired a positive value, life became dynamic.

What people want to get away from when they want to "get away from it all" is history (guilt, suffering, the changing). Where they flee to—Hawaii, the ocean beaches, the lakes and mountains—is the cosmos (innocence, paradise, the changeless). History is often bad news, and most people try to stay out of its way if they can; for some, on the other hand, it is not only excitement and adventure, but the actual biography of humanity, in which mishaps and tragedies, as in individual life, are the principal means by which we learn the truth about ourselves and the world: "history-making" is the supreme positive term for them. History is cities, and intellectuals (invention): the cosmos is the country, the peasants (tradition).

The cosmos is the realm of *law*. People's role there is *fulfillment through submission*. (Islam means "submission.") Their task is to get into harmony, to discover the identity between the inner world and the outer world, and to travel the spiritual path that leads to oneness with God or the divine powers. It is the realm of reverence, acceptance, humility, transcendence, continuity, peace, certitude, purity, permanence, awe, truth, great forces and energies. It is also the realm of remorseless destiny, blind fate, the wrath of the gods and infinite indifference. Its ultimate wisdom in the spiritual universe of the Abrahamic monotheisms is: "Thy will be done," and (for they are different) in the spiritual universe of the East: "Lead me from the unreal to the real." The apprentice to the former wisdom must learn faith and submission; the apprentice to the latter must learn detachment, renunciation, the extinction of the ego.

History is the realm of *freedom*: the goal which people involved in history are often fighting to attain or defend is freedom. Their role in that realm is *creativity*: imagination, curiosity, audacity, intervention, discovery, exploration, conquest and mastery. It is the realm of change, relativity, restlessness, aspiraticn, instability, agitation, enthusiasm and disillusion, triumph and disaster. Its ultimate wisdom is: "Onward!"

Defenders of the cosmos argue that historical freedom is really servitude, at least for the overwhelming majority of humanity, and that cosmic submission is freedom: "Thy will is our peace." Defenders of history, on the other hand, maintain that traditional societies perpetuated oppressive class relationships, in which the servitude of a majority insured the material comfort and cultural privileges of a parasitical elite who promulgated the doctrine of "cosmic submission" within a "natural order of things" for obvious reasons; in this view the basic indictment of traditional societies is that they were undemocratic: the democratic ideal is at the heart of historical progressivist ideologies. It follows that cosmic submission (or philosophic detachment or resignation or acceptance), from the historical point of view, is at best passivity, at worst a selfish evasion of responsibility amounting to actual complicity with evil.

The cosmos addresses the individual, the soul. Its social doctrine, stressing virtues rather than systems, teaches that individual transformation, through the observance of revealed or traditional precepts and the imitation of exemplary people, the saints, is the basis of earthly felicity, or that earthly felicity is actually a will-o-the-wisp and ethical purity should be regarded as an offering, a sacrifice of the ego, an end in itself, marking the precondition for sanctity or divine union. History, on the other hand, addresses the citizen. It is the arena of the masses: the masses, or at least so they are told, especially in revolutionary times, make history. The goal of their endeavor is the social order allowing for a maximum of freedom, equality, creativity and material well-being. As makers and products of history they are compelled to believe that their labor has meaning, that life is both improvable and improving. The axiom of the historical realm, therefore, is progress.

History offers *hope*, and therefore it encourages action. Within historical reality people live in the perennial hope of better times to come, for themselves or for their children; their participation in public life, in its struggles and campaigns, in war or in peace, is fed by hope, a hope which realizes its ultimate form in the dream of the Messiah. As the realm of hope, it is also the realm of despair. The cosmos, on the other hand, offers *answers*, and therefore it encourages contemplation. It is the realm of the inner Path, the Way that leads to illumination, salvation and peace; the alternative is continual rebirth, or history. The historical enterprise elicits participation by offering hope, the cosmos removes hope by convincing people in the course of time that it is an illusion. History is perpetually reinvigorated by new generations eager to embrace hope: the cosmos leaves those who arrive at disillusionment no choice but the worship, adoration and praise of God. History is the realm of soaring idealism (naivete from the cosmic perspective); the cosmos is the realm of sober realism (cynicism from the historical perspective). Although all revelations contain all the divine moments, in historical societies God tends to be seen as movement, power, will and love, immanent and personal, whereas in cosmic societies God tends to be seen as truth, reality, knowledge and witness, transcendent and impersonal.

In the cosmos people flow with the river: in history they dam it up, divert it and, quite often, pollute it. History is drama: "the tumult and the shouting." The cosmos is stillness: "the silent stars go by." History invites people into venture, trial and enterprise: the cosmos appeals to their longing for peace. In history the subject and object of love is humanity: in the cosmos the subject and object of love is God, and humanity *in* God. (From the cosmic point of view, to love humanity in itself, separate from God, to elevate the relative to the level of the absolute and make of it an autonomous object of sacrifice and adoration, is idolatry.) The cosmos teaches people to find truth in themselves, in the kingdom within (spirit), while history urges them to find truth, as justice, in movements and ideologies, in particular nations and their particular histories, in the kingdoms outside them (matter), and ultimately in the total human enterprise. The cosmos emphasizes being, history emphasizes doing. When Lenin said "Truth is what's good for the revolution" he was proclaiming his solidarity with history (the ephemeral, the relative, the world). When Jesus, Who was the Christ, said "I am the Way and the Truth and the Life" he was referring to cosmic reality, to Himself (the enduring, the absolute, God), or His eternal birth, as the revelatory Will from which the cosmos proceeds.

From the historical point of view cosmic realities are merely subjective, figments of the imagination, the indulgences of an inner life having literally the same reality as a dream: they are "all in your head." From the cosmic point of view the most that can be said of historical realities is that they come and they go: to define oneself by the ephemeral is to become ephemeral, whereas to disengage oneself from it, to discover what is enduring, is to discover reality and become real.

But points of view are affairs of the mind. In the act of living, in life not as it is known but as it is lived, the Two are really One.

The Boundary:
Liberated Psychology

Introduction

Amy Rosenblatt was sixth on the program. Born in 1933, she received her M.D. from Albert Einstein College of Medicine in 1962 and a Ph.D in Psychology from UCLA in 1971. She is currently on the faculty of Michigan State University.

Dr. Rosenblatt is a tall, almost gaunt woman who appeared to be in ill health at the time of the Conference. As her paper is poetic her reading was dramatic. In her introductory remarks, whose style of terse precision was in startling contrast to the almost Shakespearean style of her delivery, she described *The Boundary* as "an extended definition of a reality resistant to explication in discursive prose."

Dr. Rosenblatt's paper possesses the triple merits of literary style, profundity and impracticality referred to in the Introduction. I also chose it for inclusion in this volume because, while remaining essentially psychological, it manages nonetheless to expand psychology's domain to include those aspects of life whose absence or reduction, or even invalidation, in psychological literature has often been pointed out by critics of the discipline. In her own words again, "Psychology is not descriptive, it is normative—by which I mean inseparable from our ethical being; it is not autonomous, it is intended—by which I mean rooted in a consciousness of human destiny; and it doesn't take place in your head, it takes place in the universe—by which I mean that the self does not end at the skin, that we are more than what we appear to be, that traditional psychology is flawed at its very center, in its definition of identity." Finally, this paper is a statement of hope. In its closing section it becomes

clear that Dr. Rosenblatt has been presenting us not only
with a perspective but with what she regards as a solution,
"impractical" to be sure, of the crisis—at least in its specifically American contours.

    The Boundary inspired the following passage in my journal:

> *To withhold oneself or not to withhold oneself: that is the
> question.*
>
> *There was something exaggerated, I believe, in Dr. Rosen-
> blatt's paper. Perhaps immature would be a better word. I
> believe we outgrow the social imperative, the demand that we
> identify with and give ourselves to "humanity" as a whole,
> involving ourselves in its "causes"—or should I say its Cause?
> Dr. Rosenblatt, with perhaps a certain degree of unconscious
> manipulation, is pleading for community, for communion,
> as a solution to our personal and collective crisis. A powerful
> argument, to be sure. I'm certain Martin Buber would have
> nodded his head throughout. Jesus also.*
>
> *. . . I have lived a private life, hewn my own path. People
> like me do not save worlds. I have no answer to Dr. Rosen-
> blatt's argument, nor do I think there is any. We may save
> ourselves as individuals, but we can only save ourselves collec-
> tively by acting in concert. This would seem to be true, but I
> believe it is perhaps not so simple. Most of what we have done
> "in concert" has been destructive, whereas the creative main-
> tenance of the world and of individual felicity seems to depend
> on each fulfilling his responsibility without submerging his
> uniqueness in a collective identity, the fate of so many in
> modern mass societies. Are we one or are we many? Clearly
> we are both; perhaps that's the crux of our dilemma.*
>
> *Dr. Rosenblatt's paper seems to demand that we take risks.
> I have been, I hope, a generous man, prudent without being
> calculating, and nobody's fool. To take risks without prior
> circumspection is simply despair; I've seen people go under on
> that path. The paper is disturbing, however, in the way that life
> itself is disturbing. It reminds us that we never, or very rarely
> and briefly, feel that nothing more is required of us, that all is*

well. Our destiny is always 'beyond' us. She draws us toward the dynamic aspect of life, the ever-questing, ever-growing, ever-evolving and ever-uncertain aspect of ourselves, at the expense, I think, of that inner peace and contentment, which is basically humility, that seems to become increasingly important and increasingly accessible as we grow older, and which is equally fundamental to our nature. She is summoning us, in Dr. Frank's terminology, to confront our historical dimension, which is doubtless one of our responsibilities, at the expense of the cosmic. The public at the expense of the personal, the life of the citizen at the expense of the life of the soul. An error of imbalance, and of youth.

I have heard that summons before. To what extent I have heeded it is not for me, or anyone, to say. If we are to be judged, then so be it: I have not tried to escape. And I have faced my abyss.

Later: Upon reading the transcript of Dr. Rosenblatt's paper I realize that I may have underestimated her philosophical acumen. It is difficult to be certain, given the deliberate ambiguity of her style, but here and there in her paper, and especially in sections 10, 11 and 12, there seem to be intimations of our cosmic invariables, although the historical dimension is definitely accorded ultimate primacy, indeed celebrated, in her concluding section. There is, it would appear, a balance in the dynamism she extols with such rapture. But no respite.

The Boundary:
Liberated Psychology

by Amy Rosenblatt

What's our first step?
Choosing a direction
How do we choose a direction?
The direction is always given. We move towards the boundary.
What is the boundary?
That has always been the question.
We begin, then, as we have always begun: by confronting the mystery of
the boundary.

In our first weeks we stare intently at patches of light and color. Our head, the cumbersome servant of our searching gaze, turns slowly, nodding unsteadily on the frail tendons. We peer in calm amazement at the unfolding world. Consciousness, as yet formless and unretentive, unaware even of itself, foreshadows nonetheless from the outset its inherent spirit of approach. Anticipation, expectant curiosity and the intuition of growth and purpose, discernible only to the adult equipped with those very faculties, are already prophetic in our wide, unblinking and fathomless eyes, already unmistakable, their presence so early in life rendered vivid, even awesome, by contrast with the helplessness of their possessor. The shape of our awareness, even before we can think, points us toward the boundary.

We are launched, then, from the beginning, inescapably and in every moment. But the boundary can only be reached in freedom. We are seekers after truth. Protagonists. Creators.

1.

In social situations we have to be on guard; it's in our relationships, from the intimate to the historical, that the real ground is gained or lost. But when we're alone, focussed, pensive, escaped from the pressures, nothing at stake, we often wander toward the boundary.

With each step a crust of the public self drops away, until nothing remains but that troubled honesty, exiled in daily life to the role of a helpless witness, whose observations we always deliberately disfigure by delivering them with grating irony or an exaggerated harshness, as if to shield its purity from ridicule or minimize the depth of our concern. But now we are at one with it; we allow it to lead us where it will. Our state of mind becomes fluid. Serenity and terror, detachment and intensity, anger and compassion loom and dissolve like dancers in fantastically hodgepodge dress, unified despite their incongruity by the eerie unerring magic of the dance. Closeness to the boundary is frightening and comforting at the same time, frightening because it awakens within us a conflict between terrible urgency and total hopelessness, and comforting because we sense the pressure of a deep truth or reality, a warning or prophecy from a being committed to us more deeply and surely than we are ourselves. Sometimes we stumble back sick with despair, sometimes we merely lapse into melancholy; sometimes, because the boundary replenishes our self-respect and liberates us from trivial worries and doubts, we enjoy renewed strength.

The person we become in solitary communion near the boundary is, we feel and hope, our true self. We conceal it from others because they wouldn't understand, but if they knew this real self, we tell ourselves, they'd respect us more than they do, listen to our advice, maybe even love us; they'd realize that the person they believe us to be is really a composite of necessary reactions to unavoidable situations, merely a role we play. Sometimes, when sufficiently provoked or yielding to a perverse impulse, we allow a moment of the real self to flash out, as a test, never going so far that we won't be able to disclaim it all later with a disgusted shrug. But it doesn't work. Just when we most want to be acknowledged, if not as recipients of revelation at least as sincere, we're invariably misunderstood, our moment of genuineness impatiently degraded by that automatic repudiation of the boundary which is always boring, infuriating or pathetic. After awhile, usually in our mid-thirties, we give up; the address from the boundary diminishes to a fleeting inscrutable detachment from the conversation or the task at hand.

Each of us suspects at times that the boundary exists only in his or her own mind, a private fantasy. At other times, when we look closely at people and actually try to imagine the grain and texture of their experience, the expressions on their faces when they're alone, their secret world, when we empathize without passing judgment, we have no doubt that they're all thinking the same thing.

2.

In crowds a great temptation to approach the boundary tantalizes our souls. We're all strangers, all anonymous, there couldn't be any unpleasant consequences; if it became awkward we would just smile and walk away, guiltlesss, richly amused and slightly dizzy. We feel that shared proximity to the boundary, even only for a moment, would be unforgettable, truly mystical, the very goal of life.

But we rarely make the attempt; if at all, half-heartedly. The bright smile, or the smile of composure with which we establish our claim to worldliness, sticks to our faces no matter what we say. Or our manner betrays a certain calculating prudence, readily perceived by others. In any case, we lower our sights, with little regret because our hopes were never very high.

The power of the boundary is in our minds, but its source and effect are in the world. It seems to be within us but it's really between us. It's real. There's no personal failure if we grow tired or cynical or lose our nerve. There is a failure, but it isn't personal.

3.

The concept of distance from the boundary has many interpretations, all valid at the same time even though they are contradictory; our effort to comprehend the boundary must be as subtle, manifold and paradoxical as the boundary itself. We've always known this, just as we've always known that the boundary is something like a mind, and can only be understood, therefore, by entering it. Distance from or within a mind resists measurement. But the vocabulary of distance is the only one that works.

Because our life energy flows into us from the boundary, we feel something stretching thin and threatening to tear as we withdraw from it, something alive like flesh, capable of experiencing pain and relief. In this aspect, we become more aware of it as we recede. An anxious restlessness invades our surprised endeavor, or mysterious lethargy, or desperation.

In another aspect, the boundary only has two moments, distance and proximity; distance occurs when we forget it, proximity when we remember. If we've been distant from it for any length of time, and then suddenly remember it, we feel empty, as if we'd wasted our lives or been childish; we were empty all along and hadn't known it. Our awareness of the boundary when we have forgotten it is an accumulating emptiness, experienced as an inability to concentrate.

Closeness to the boundary may produce opposite reactions. Sometimes when we look reality in the face we feel a sense of peace, sometimes a sense of imprisonment; in both cases the journey to the boundary brings a liberation from illusions. As it always does.

Finally, we can also be distant from it and fully conscious of the distance, as of an inner abyss whose merciless reaches separate us from our true selves. In bitterness, for example, or in hatred of life, or in fear.

4.

Our longing to approach the boundary can be debased and manipulated, because our knowledge of it is so vague; all we know, or believe we know, is that events unfold and erupt there with that greater intensity and immediate significance we usually associate with adventure, disaster or warfare; life, and therefore death, are vivid there. Our intuition of the boundary can degenerate into a fascination with spectacles, an indiscriminate hunger for excitement. We line up at the stadium or the movies prepared to enter a domain where things actually happen; decisions and actions make a difference, the stakes are obvious. We don't care if it's all unreal; all we care about is the experience, the hour or two of escape from routine, the thrilling encounter between courage and danger.

When we return from a spectacle, our daily lives re-emerge through the descending reverberations and fading flares of colorful action exactly as they always were, solid as stone, unchanged and unmarked; we have no new perspective on them, and this is as we want it to be. The resumption of routine falls gradually upon us like the comfort of a familiar blanket bringing warmth and sleep; we feel drained of tension and grateful for renewed predictability. It's reassuring to re-enter, to find everything just as we left it. We stroll home laughing and sighing.

But when we return from the boundary we know something real has happened. If we want peace of mind we just have to wait for it. The contours of the routine leap out at us now like the furnishings of a room in which the lights have suddenly been snapped on, stunning, transparent and finally vulnerable, every detail rigid with staggering significance to which we are customarily, and unbelievably, blind.

5.

We are reluctant to approach the boundary with others, even though all life draws us toward it, because we know that once the journey to the boundary has been shared, by any number of people, something must follow, some form of mutual commitment, whether to openness or action, which would entail risk. The shorter the distance from the boundary—of an event, a moment, an insight, whatever— the higher its priority; the boundary has about it the aura of a vow, of surrender, of irreversible decision. One moment shared at the boundary could claim precedence over our entire previous life. If we didn't follow through, our reputations would be cheapened. We would be branded hypocrites. In some sense, obscure at first but growing clearer with the passage of time, we would be damned.

Our first judgments of people, no matter what their form, are often unconscious assessments of the likelihood of shared approach to the boundary, or at least of how near we might be able to go; we also try to imagine the quality of it, the style, flavor and emphasis, because no two experiences at the boundary are ever the same, and all of them summarize both the unique unrepeatable fullness of that particular moment in the cosmos and the entire previous lives of the people involved. But because we are ambivalent about the boundary, we're sometimes made uneasy by the very qualities—sincerity, seriousness, depth—which indicate one kind of knowledge of it (there are other kinds) and forecast progressively frequent returns. People who've found freedom at the boundary, who habitually stand at it observing others in secret, allowing themselves to be possessed by its power of vision, are unpredictable, even unstable, because they're aware of an unnamed priority higher than usefulness or security.

6.

Distance from the boundary varies throughout the day, sometimes as rapidly as the flickering reflections with which water answers wind and light, each movement seeming, also like the reflection, to be an answer of the organism to presences, conscious and impalpable, whose impersonal urgency contains full knowledge of our most intimate history. In the restless solitude of our stream of consciousness we veer toward and away from it with each change of mood.

But distance from the boundary is never definite or numerical, never a fact. Immersed in the drowsy incoherence of reverie, for example, when we allow our thoughts to pursue without interference their constantly uncompleted sequences, awareness of the boundary persists as a faint nagging in the back of our minds, like the punctuated roar of artillery heard from far away; when we abruptly and impatiently turn our attention to it, finally unable to ignore it, we realize that it's nothing less than the immense tenacious reality of our own lives—or of the larger life that contains us, compounded of history, the planet and the cosmic insurgence—conscious of insult and demanding respect. Sometimes we're able to recall that a part of our mind was focussed on it all along, tugging tirelessly at the fringes of the reverie in which we had hoped to find refuge from a suspicion whose proof or disproof we were too exhausted, or too cynical, to seek any longer, or a challenge too confusing to understand, much less confront. One part of our minds is always drawn toward the boundary, another is always trying to pretend it doesn't exist; stretched out on the tension between the two we are uneasy, apologetic and vaguely guilt-ridden, simmering with schemes or systematically pursuing oblivion.

This entire drama takes place within a zone whose distance from the boundary is different for each of us. One person's wrenching breakthrough toward the boundary may be another's nearly forgotten childhood intuition, although the meaning of these episodes may later be redefined; no statements about the boundary are ever final, even appeals to the clearly remembered past, because the boundary reaches into our lives from outside of time. The meaning of the past changes as it is caught up in the dynamic of the present; nothing is ever settled and nothing ever dies. The music already performed gives meaning to each new note, but each new note reaches back into the past and adds new meaning to the music already performed. Truth is not contained in time, but rather contains time within it.

In our relationships with others, our distance from the boundary may be a calculated strategy, requiring constant alertness and sensitivity, or, among close friends and loved ones, a deeply habitual assumption by which the very self is defined, and in which transgression always threatens to precipitate a crisis which will bring us closer to the boundary, either in the resulting confrontation or in later solitude. Routine social situations, whether at work or with intimate friends, tend to establish the limits of a shared zone; our moods are frequently determined by the anticipation or apprehension with which we travel from zone to zone. Any gesture suggesting greater openness, a turn toward the boundary, or any retreat into greater formality, a turn away from the boundary, is immediately noted and, in proportion to its degree, must be interpreted; the increased acceptance and affirmation we long for demands reciprocity, and therefore challenges our vitality, while rejection justifies a request for an explanation. Openness enlarges the shared world, formality contracts it into the frozen patterns by which our humanity sustains itself, not without nobility, when growth is neither possible nor necessary.

We tend to spend time among people whose public zone of distance from the boundary, their "life style," is about the same as our own. True distance from the boundary, however, in the mercurial self-deceiving privacy of the mind, is a secret which cannot be deduced from outward behavior, where it is determined by class background, conscious decision, social habits and the pressures of situations; all of us have been much closer to the boundary than our visible manner, even among intimates, would indicate. It's even possible that everyone has gone all the way, if only for a blinding instant or in a dream; although there is only one boundary, it has a different meaning for each of us. In the presence of birth or death, for example, two occasions on which we avoid glimpses of the boundary only with difficulty, we discover in each other a depth of expression and maturity of contemplated experience formerly veiled or even dissembled because nothing in life seemed to elicit it.

In our struggle to understand our lives, distance from the boundary is a metaphor, an approximation to something that escapes definitive statement. But in the great ground of things it is reality itself. Closeness to the boundary is measured by knowledge of its meaning: knowledge of its meaning is a way of life, a single action sustained across the life span. Those we remember, who inspire us, are those who saw it and knew what it was. Their exultant clarity of vision embodied itself as devotion to the rest of us. Those who've truly been to the boundary always return. They walk among us, they celebrate the way, they uplift our spirits. What they learn at the boundary is the love of humanity.

7.

The world as it appears when we have forgotten the boundary requires no interpretation and leads only back into itself. Its drama is either accepted at face value or scorned as a hypocritical pretense, confirming the "basic selfishness" of human nature, in which all are compelled to play a role, and in which only the most shallow or gullible take their parts seriously. For each private ambition the stakes are high, and we feel deeply engaged; in any other sense nothing matters at all, and we laugh cynically. When we forget the boundary we lose hope of any perspective more elevated than individual self-interest and of any vision more penetrating than the one which skims the surface; from this worm's-eye view our enslavement to the inhuman laws which dictate the movement of objects—laws which, in this society, are economic—remains invisible. We play the game.

The boundary forgotten, we throw ourselves into life with the single-minded eagerness we note lovingly in children and point to as characteristically human, determined not to miss out on a fulfillment never clearly defined, but whose reality, nonetheless, cannot be challenged. The images of satisfied faces smiling triumphantly at us from all sides are proof. They arouse our envy and stimulate our competitive performance. What the world seems to offer is a million varieties of happiness, a profusion of delectable choices for every appetite. The more money we have, the more happiness we can buy.

But it doesn't work. Everything, eventually, becomes boring: worn out, as if it had a startlingly brief life span impossible to foresee in the stirring kinetic vigor of its initial leap into our lives. Ungratefully disrupting the serenity or well-being purchased in good faith, our minds wander and contaminate, with restlessness and vague desperation, the victory that seemed so certain when we planned it. The old troublesome and enigmatic uneasiness returns, unanswerable as ever. Staring into space, we smoke cigarettes to focus our irritated concentration, but we lose our train of thought anyway; we feel inexplicably, and very purely, sad. Before others, and to a degree before ourselves, we sustain the pretense of a successful life and wonder whether others sustain the same pretense before us, whether they also live in two worlds and don't know which one is real. We're never certain. If the public world is real, why can't we find each other in it? If the private world is real, if our suspicions are substantiated, what prevents us from speaking of it, from sharing it?

We have turned toward the boundary again, dimly aware that the only solution to the mystery of our emptiness and loneliness awaits us in that direction, and that the first step is some kind of admission or confession. But admissions and confessions are the fragile offspring of trust, and who can we trust? If we've succeeded in following the thought through this far, the apprehension of shame conquers our souls. Easier to conclude it's all nonsense, some quirk of the mind. Win a few, lose a few. We look for someone with whom we can share warmth, a kind moment, a simple plea-sure whose time-honored successful indulgence guarantees that there will be no unpredictable consequences. We re-enter the stream of things, feeling a weary but renewed hope. We try to forget what happened, sometimes forget our whole lives, and start fresh.

8.

Fear lies in wait at the boundary. Hunched forward through yellowish gloom, it leers at our hesitant approach as if taunting the conflicted motivations, and resulting weak-ness of purpose, that will make us an easy prey. Drawing near, we stare ahead as if hypnotized, our minds racing. The view from the boundary pierces through the surface of things to the horror we usually refer to only obliquely, or ironically, in tones of tired familiar disgust whose undercurrent of impatience betrays an innocence that shrank back, rather than that deliberate detachment from weakening emotions which we acquire only after taking foolish risks, plunging into life and suffering without squirming, and with faith. If we're overwhelmed by fear, we'll see only the horror, not the totality which gives it meaning and holds out hope, and the horror will be all we'll remember. Unless we become conscious of the miscarriage, we'll be possessed by fear. A part of us will always be locked in the endless moment in which we stood transfixed, as if helplessly collaborating with an irresistible intuition or sense of retribution by which we knew precisely the length of time necessary, between the initial paralyzing shock and the wail of tearing loose, for the vision to be seared into our brains forever.

The journey to the boundary is a rite of passage. If the rite is interrupted at the climax, we cannot scurry back as if nothing had happened. Terrified revulsion, a life of flight and denial, are signs of a mutilated vision that can only be made whole through liberation of the love whose defeat by fear at the crucial moment was the disaster which interrupted the rite. Fear is one of the very great powers. The passionate inflexible denial of ugliness, precisely because it is also knowledge, rages in us as a spiritual hysteria that isolates the soul, which becomes repulsive to itself and opaque to the bewildered overtures of others. We become calculating and manipulative but remain innocent, a form of treachery which eats away at the very center of selfhood. In this state, we dwell upon love, pure outpouring love, as if hovering over a fetish, crooning and moaning to it, imploring its intercession with an urgency barely concealing the struggle against suicide silently engaged in the background like the coiled frozen embrace of equally matched wrestlers, locked motionless with every muscle taut.

Once fear possesses us at the boundary it never leaves us until loneliness drives us back. The more cunning our evasion, the more we prolong the pain. But it does happen; we recover. After tossing in anguish we finally fall asleep near dawn, and when we awaken, for a reason we'll never know, the calm is in the room. Healed by that final surrender of the separate self which is also called the grace of God, we finally accept the simple fact that there are good and evil in this world, and a true path nonetheless, and even, restored to us at last after such long hunger and sorrow, the wild sweet excitement in the smell of the rain. We come home. What we see from the boundary is home. No matter what it is, it's home.

9.

The boundary is not that burst of release where we "pour our hearts out." It isn't the crumpled midnight where we divulge our petty shameful secrets and give vent to the celebrated pent-up feelings which always appear so disturbingly trivial in their revelation, until we realize, in later ironic reappraisal, that their triviality was the very reason we wanted so desperately to liberate ourselves from them. As we approach the boundary, the ambitions of our personal life shrivel and collapse, like paper in a fire; they lose their power to dominate our consciousness and persuade us that they are our only hope. When we realize that nothing of the personal past is our own but our responsibilities, we raise our eyes toward the boundary. Only there, our souls burned clean, can we find a purpose and communion worthy of that latent devotion whose frustration was the real root of humiliation and emptiness.

The pouring out of our hearts is a device, contrived by the soul's unfailing intuition, to expose the myth of a private fate and liberate us for travel toward the boundary. Toward others. Toward contact.

10.

Rainbow-colored, descending like an immense blade or advancing edge, cleaving through every event, every moment and every mind, the boundary arches through the universe, the perpetual horizon of all things created. From the teeming flagellants bubbling in the hot froth of microbiotic life, to the stars poised and gleaming in their unmoving and unimaginable velocities, diamonds of fire, all things hurl themselves toward the image they see in it, their own image.

"At work" in America our continuous intuition of the boundary, as so often in extremity, is reduced to a simple-minded passion for escape; we become the pure will to freedom, a component of the human essence, and one of our great powers, but devoid of content. In this state, the boundary seems to close in and wrap itself around us like a second skin, crushing us inward with intimate brutality. The voice of work, like an iron god announcing the single rule of some diabolical game, intones: This is hell and death, everything else is freedom. The lifeless objects around us, bolted to the walls and floors, share dumbly our misery, slaves to the same implacable power. On the harder days, every thought as it enters our minds thrusts forward, in haggard outrage, an invitation to shatter the moment. Most of the time, in sincere absorption and with loving atention to detail, we leaf methodically through the strange childlike fantasies whose power and reliability have been proved through the years. Another escape.

But every now and then something else happens. We become suddenly detached from the wild subterranean impulse to burst loose; it remains, but we regard it dispassionately, curiously, as only one element among others in a problem just revealed to our eyes. The surge and lull of fantasy sputters to a halt, its emptiness as clear as the guilt in the blinking sheepish smile of an imposter whose mask is suddenly snatched away. We look up from the task—wearily, with that intensity of inner focus never seen on the Earth but in the eyes of human beings, that intensity before which the whole universe, wondering and expectant, falls into silent motionless respect, look up as if dimly groping for some truth as incredible as the fact that it was forgotten, and ask ourselves, finally under heaven to what end we labor. Then we have arrived at the truth. Then we stand at the boundary.

11.

Like a magnet whose substance and power of attraction is thought itself, the boundary tirelessly pulls us toward the fearless honesty which, pronounced in word or act, becomes the center upon which all eyes suddenly are rivetted: the moment when the spell is broken, as with a magic wand, the frozen figures leap to life, and the world, in fierce elation, bursts through its crust of doubt, released.

But we resist the pull. The tension tightening in the room when we are talking "small talk," for example, is resistance. So is that watchful prudence with which we stifle briskly the impulse to generosity that flares up from time to time behind our daily facade, disturbing with intimations of pettiness, or cowardice, our equable commitment to maintain appearances at all costs. So is the ugly joke or sadistic innuendo with which we vulgarize our lives, the vicious lightning response to tentative gestures of trust whose aftertaste of self-hatred, like a drug, overwhelms our lame attempt to figure out what on Earth got into us. So is our reluctance to "get involved."

We resist the pull of the boundary in a thousand ways, and by our very nature: by the slowness of our evolution, by our fear of losing the precarious advantages we've gained, by the myriad illusions of the ego, by our unconscious performance of self-destructive social roles. Yet at the same time, so powerful is our vision, so compelling the truth we glimpse at the boundary, we're convinced that if the conditions were right we could truly triumph over that nature, over the indigenous mortal flaws—the wound of malice, the drag of matter, the Ignorance, the Old Adam—whose baleful inheritance we detected and fought from the beginning, and so bravely. We have that triumph before us: that much can be said. Our faith rises, our faith falls.

But everything leads to the boundary. Love, work, child-rearing, aging, thinking, worshipping. Every endeavor, every process, every desire. If we persevere long enough at anything we hear its call and realize we've been hearing it all along: our lives, whether as resistance or ambivilence or jubilant acquiescence, were all along a reply to its ageless calm hypnotic proposal.

We hear it most clearly, of course, when our determination is challenged by the inescapable treachery of every path. Anger or uncertainty or both may sweep us off into frightened solitude; the people whose encouragement validated our lives may suddenly become evasive before our spontaneous confidence; the world we built in honest sacrifice may turn against us, a nightmare whispering obscenity into our ears; the mysterious icy ambiguity slithers into our self-assurance like a reptile at the last moment, when we're least prepared for a reversal, when we thought we had the real answer at last, and shame lowers our eyes before the nervous embarrassment of our friends; what once stood the test so well now fails. And if nothing overt jostles our equilibrium there's always the haunting uncertainty swirling lazily, in sinister constancy, even within our most praiseworthy self-denial; we confront it every time we contemplate the next step. At these moments of crisis in the drama, if our courage prevails, we turn toward the boundary. Healing and strengthening, it summons forth the creative purpose whose loss confirmed the failure, orienting our souls to that perpetual self-transcendence in which humanity recognizes its style and celebrates its return of the gift.

Everything leads to the boundary. The point, however, is not that resistance is futile because the boundary's power asserts itself inevitably, but rather that it's suicidal. We have the power to resist. We're familiar with that collapse of purpose which is the specifically human hell.

Resistance to the pull of the boundary is what we call anxiety. The deliverance from anguish is rebirth. We're pulled toward rebirth, we resist because we fear death. But death and rebirth are the way of the world. The path to the boundary.

12.

Drawn to the boundary by a force as constant as the force of gravity, our own love of life, we yield up to a certain point and then resist. The drama of our lives, which is the drama of the cosmic evolution, is played out at the point of resistance. What the heart redeems as poignant and the mind seizes upon as significant is the perspective we gain from the unrealized potential just beyond that point, and the deepest love of our lives, the love that saves and never dies, the true love of humanity unquenchable in all of us, is the love of that drama.

Although the invariable common denominator in our moments of resistance is fear, there is no end to our repertoir of styles and strategies. Individual or conspiratorial, habitual or deliberate, contrived in freedom or in servitude to convention, they are the dynamic in a private biography we share with few or none.

We often smile at people, for example, just to reassure them that we're all right. We catch their eye just long enough to flash the bright proof of our undaunted bravery, relieving them of their burden of concern and then return, because there's no social sanction to procede further, to the forlorn reveries in which we recall images, but not the flavor, of the spontaneity we enjoyed before the doors began to close one by one leaving us finally no alternative to subservience. Later that night we wonder, depressed by the emptiness of our speculation, if they had an intuition of the response we simultaneously entreated and prevented, knowing it was unthinkable under the circumstances, and shared our feeling of helpless immobility. We fall asleep resigned again.

The defensive alertness darting from threat to threat behind our most convincing self-assurance also is resistance, in the form of a refusal to admit the unexamined further possibilities of our character. Even when we have imagined these possibilities ourselves, we hide behind the boisterous or sophisticated impostures that proclaim our contentment with completed lives. The move toward the boundary, toward growth, always means relinquishing a position we've conquered through jealous tenacity, with no guarantee, or even clear definition, of vindication. Saving face is understandable.

The adroit dissimulations of our eager wit and exaggerated sympathy are techniques with which we decline or forestall the offer of genuine solidarity, which is always an offer to move together toward the boundary. Something else could have been said; an honest proposal, conveyed with courteous respect throughout a long friendship, could have been acknowledged and accepted, but we were afraid we weren't equal to the demand. We withhold ourselves; we set limits.

Our oblique inquiries about what other people really do with their time are the cautious expression of an intense covert curiosity, tinged with fear, that weaves improbable theories through a major portion of our fantasies. Rather than risk an abortive initiative, we seek reassurance that others have not outstripped us. Similarly, the false gusto with which we plead for envy of our lives is a technique to discourage or mislead the honest scrutiny necessary for growth. An indulgence in slander or a flight into pretense—or even worse, into pretension—is always a refusal to move toward the boundary.

Finally our resistance is revealed, and our awareness of the summons is betrayed, in our confusion and evasiveness, our irritation or shame, when some intrusion into the routine or some unexpected twist in a conversation suddenly menaces our secrets or challenges our maneuvers. The distance is kept with deadly seriousness. We change the subject, deftly, pointedly if necessary, or bridge the awkward rift with self-conscious laughter, repressing the urge to assess with a glance the level of recovery. Sometimes we become angry, but never with a clear conscience.

The attitudes and techniques by which we maintain our chosen distance from the boundary betray our awareness of its call. Resigned to its indestructible presence and power, we respond faithfully, with ecstasy, calm joy, grudging submission, prudent disavowal or blind flight, to its disquieting and vaguely thrilling invitation.

It isn't as if we know what's there and deliberately hold back, choosing instead to bargain for ambiguous partial advantages. We are guiltless in our ingenious diplomacy with the boundary. We really don't know what awaits us there, or why we sometimes resist its summons, even in those lucid moments when we recognize it as our love of life, and at other times hurl ourselves toward its beckoning energy like prisoners toward their freedom. Those who've travelled there, without exception, preface their reports with the disclaimer that it cannot really be known except by direct experience. Nor is it an apocalypse; we return and carry on. We just know, with a conviction as ancient as the memory in our genes, that there's something dangerous about the boundary. It exacts payment for mistakes.

We aren't actually conscious of the boundary as a bound-

ary, of course. We only recognize, in the fateful moment
when our strength of will gives out, an old familiar alarm,
vague and piercing at once, and the skilled reflexes of the
mind, at home in patterns of evasion and retreat established
over a lifetime, swifty carry us back into the safe circum-
scribed mechanical reality of our social roles.

13.

The boundary sometimes takes on the semblance of an
internal terrain.

In certain of our moods it appears ominous. Patches of
darkness glide steadily, like cloud shadows, across the margin observing our cautious advance; the margin itself, jagged
and murky, is blown with mist, shifting shades of green and
flashes of harsh weak light. Half-visible forms, suggesting
ruins or battlements, loom through tendrils of fog. Everything is silent.

We imagine, stretching beyond, a radioactive wasteland:
glowing lifeless reaches of fused rock and soil reeking, mile
upon mile, to a shapeless horizon where a last few bombs still
explode in the insane overkill we have learned to accept, and
anticipate, as simply one more part of the grim picture, its
logical culmination. We try to envision the final moments
preceding the suicide. Chaos, terrified pointless flight,
spasms of murderous hatred, islands of prayer. This is a
possiblility.

In one of its dimensions the boundary is purely temporal
and presents to us, in images of unmistakable clarity and
force, the fears and hopes which provoke our visions of the
future. We are all mental survivors of Hiroshima. The
mushroom cloud rears as vivid and archetypal before us now
as the sunrise, the mother or the Cross. The boundary
reveals to us all our potentials, the complete range of choice;
it respects and guarantees the completeness of our freedom

and, whether we like it or not, of our responsibility as well. The macabre humor we project into this thoroughness is really an ironic recognition on our own part of our inveterate but futile reluctance to confront our destiny: a part of us would always just like to crawl away somewhere and stagnate, but we know we can't.

The terrains unfolding in our minds, therefore, are not always menacing. We also imagine, sometimes, beyond the jagged margin, which could symbolize a great ordeal or conflict, the rolling plains and teeming life of an Earth intact, even resurrected, in all its majesty. The rumbling herds of bison, the passenger pigeons darkening the air with flashing rushing wings, the whales chanting once more their ocean sagas: all that was destroyed restored. Gleaming, halcyon, the planet drifts through peace again. The myriad eyes of night, as once before, blink in the moonlight, warm, pulsing, conscious; vagrant winds murmer and sigh, deepening sleep even though unheard by the sleepers. The interrupted harmony of life and death resumes.

The boundary reveals to us all our choices, all our possibilities. But it is not neutral. No more than we are.

14.

We feel enclosed within us, mute and powerless as a swaying sea-creature rooted to the aquarium floor, another self, thwarted in every try for life by barren circumstances, hasty decisions and tricks of fate whose calamitous significance, unrecognizable at the time, had to await the painful reassessment of the person we became by default. This is the self we think of when we speculate—light-heartedly in public but quite otherwise in private—about what we would do if we had our lives to live over again. Our secret knowledge of it, bitter, sorrowful or resigned, is the call of the boundary, piercing back through memory, intention, disappointment and recovery to the center of the divine potential.

Seated carelessly somewhere in the back of our minds, discouraged, the other self suffers silently and incompletely like a child whose spirit has been broken, and we, cradling its confusion within us, must come to terms with our role. Before its imaginary judgment we want to be admired as indignant victims, keenly sensitive and defiant; guilt follows complacency surely as a shadow. We crouch over its restive and bewildered distraction as if to implore comprehension, and above all appreciation, of the waves of helpless anger that dispute our suspicious endurance of life's neutrality. We want to be innocent. And if we actually collaborated, through self-indulgence, indifference or despair, with a crime so heinous as an assault upon a self before self-awareness was mature enough to defend its promise, we want to be forgiven. This was our own being, the inviolate seed; the need to absolve ourselves of complicity becomes paramount, and if not satisfied submerges every other response. The force behind it is pride.

The boundary is the pressure of an alternative identity; the style and intensity of our relationship to it is the principle component of our personality, the constant theme tinging every trait and explaining every episode. We are a dialogue between what we are and what we feel we were meant to be. We bore people, oblivious of their polite patience, with plaintive descriptions of the injury which suddenly and tragically cut short a premature excellence heralding certain fame. Visions of our lives as a sequence of weak-willed compromises trouble our sleep. A ragged quarter of an hour, taking advantage of exhaustion, declares itself the fruit and proof of a lifetime's self-deception, and we resume our work with downcast eyes and a quizzical, faintly haggard smile. Single moments in our lives—an impetuous accusation, a failure of generosity, a timid retreat from a challenge, a character misread for unworthy reasons, a childish recrimination that should have been withheld—haunt our reveries, nagging us with pale remorse. Our lives were despoiled by marriage or its ill-advised rejection, by a childhood too pampered or too harsh, by gullibility, caution, opportunism, naivete or unwarranted resignation. None of us are exempt. We all know things could have gone otherwise. We're all familiar with envy.

The other self suppressed within us, however, cannot be described in the language of happiness or success. We think and speak of it in the social vocabulary by which the truth of our lives is obscured, but the stifled self within us, the other person who never got a chance, is an idea whose essence and ambition rebuke any attempt at parochial definition. It's neither a fixed identity nor a particular potential. It's a mode of being, a quality of life. It's participation in the cosmic evolution. The genetic possibility, isolated and therefore merely latent, is raw material for a larger purpose which fashioned it. The other self is the feeling that accompanies the conviction of being part of that purpose. Mute and powerless, it awaits the boundless energy which both emanates from the boundary and flows toward it from within us, ecstatic and uncontainable, born anew in every instant, the river of praise. Our lives are the passing waves; this we've always known, with that wild fragrant fulfilling pain, that rending cry of love in the face of death which marks our loss of innocence. But our souls, also as we've always known, with the one immemorial and amazing certainty our gratitude may cherish without fear, are the river itself. The stifled being within us is our soul: our participation in human destiny: our significance, donation and joy: the advance toward the boundary.

The boundary can call to us in the form of our devotion to an unborn self. Every attempt we make to nourish this self is a move toward the boundary. If we are beaten back repeatedly, and if a deliberate sharing of experience—classical politics, in other words: the enactment of citizenship—reveals that the outrage is endemic, then we have grounds to question the society we inhabit, because we invented society, with an unconscious intention wiser than any conscious expedient, for the precise purpose of insuring that maximum elaboration of personality which is the intrinsic goal of human evolution and the sole guarantee of its perpetually threatened continuity.

This is the procedure by which America is first unmasked. When we examine our society—its institutions and dynamics, its structure and cultural forms, its totality—in response to the call of the boundary, we realize that the force which prevents us from becoming what we were meant to be, the force which deceives our aspiration, originates there, in that society which neither reflects human intention nor addresses human potential. This truth is seen only from the boundary, because only at the boundary can we know what we were meant to be. In a sudden astounded focus upon the commonwealth, as if upon a crux of the matter which, incredibly, had never been noticed before, we find the key to the liberation of the stifled self within us. The problem is not personal. The gap between what we are and what we were meant to be can only be closed by concerted action, by that self-creation of an historical essence which shines as supreme proof of our success, by that insurgence which characterizes life in its glory. This realization, informed by the love which flows from the boundary, is the leap of human intelligence in which American society, the heartless dynamo, the fountain of endless deceptions, first becomes visible in its true significance.

The boundary is where the I and the We become fertile. Wholeness and growth, fulfillment and transcendence, the advancing light. The boundary is where the human community, in fact or in vision, is born.

Challenge of Change:
Money Versus People

Introduction

Mark William Harrison's paper was tenth on the program. Dr. Harrison was born in 1928 and received his doctorate from The London School of Economics in 1959. He is rather more inclined than the majority of his colleagues to concur with some of the conclusions of Karl Marx, and was a "radical professor" at the University of Wisconsin in Madison, one of the hotbeds of student rebellion, during the uprisings of the sixties. His books and numerous articles supported the indictment of "imperialism," and he was an outspoken critic of the Vietnam conflict. He is, in my summary, a marxist in his diagnosis and a humanist in his prescription. His perspective on the contemporary crisis was the only on at the Conference that might fairly be described as "revolutionary" in the modern specific sense of the term. That there is much more, however, than "insurgence," the term he seems to prefer, in his point of view will be quite evident to the reader.

A literary stylist like Amy Rosenblatt, Dr. Harrison also delivered his paper dramatically—that is to say, his deliberate self-restraint and matter-of-fact delivery, as well as the lucid simplicity and even understatement of the text, in their contrast with the depth and intensity of the content, established a dramatic tension in the actual reading which would be somewhat muted in the text itself. His style is spare and compressed to the point of austerity—we may recall that his field of specialization is economics—as if his sole rule in writing was to use as few words as possible; he spoke slowly and often allowed time at the end of a particularly pithy sentence for the sense to sink in. He was professorial in his manner almost to the point of haughtiness. His eyes were quick and challenging, his demeanor almost intimidating, as if he had grown accustomed to defending an unpopular position against constant assaults and had become, as a result, slightly hardened.

As I am now aware, my journal entry the night after he spoke reflects the gradual development of that personal drama alluded to in my Introduction.

> *There is little to contest in Dr. Harrison's "paper." He seems to me to present at least one possible concretization of the psychological and metaphysical scenario unveiled in* The Boundary, *and he has certainly succeeded in presenting a powerful (indeed almost belligerent) case for the humanist tradition whose disparagement in the realm of public education I have myself lamented. Money is indeed our bane, the evil spirit whose inhuman priorities permeate our society; we should not surrender to its enchantment or tolerate its dominion. Unfortunately we do.*
>
> *What the author of* Money Versus People *possesses in common with Amy Rosenblatt is an ultimate allegiance to the historical drama, to secular "truths"; their perspectives complement each other. (I keep returning to Dr. Frank's luminous distinction.) Both writers are social critics, both are activists, and both, with the best of intentions, and with almost glaringly clear consciences, are trying to convince the reader that he or she must* do *something, although exactly what is not obvious. The impact of their combined arguments—I fear they both have a bit of the ideologue in them—tends to make one feel either aloof from the great currents of modern life and therefore guilty, or aloof from the great currents of modern life and therefore fortunate. I incline to the latter—undoubtedly due to my stage of life, and also to a certain fatigue with the harangues of zealots determined to save the world. For a young man or woman, however, these papers might well provide an answer to their confusion in the chaos of contemporary society: a metaphysic, an ethic, an interpretation of history and polit-*

ics, indeed an identity—perhaps temporary, to be sure, but at least a perspective capable of carrying them a good stretch of the way to their next disillusion.

My irrepressible cynicism reasserts itself. But not, I hope, to blot out a sense of guilt. I think it becomes possible to respond cynically, in this false and treacherous world, simply to the presence of conviction, of any conviction whatever, even one with which we may feel a spontaneous sympathy. Which does not imply by any means that people of conviction are necessarily hypocritical, but rather that they are naive. Naive, and perhaps fortunate. Or, as I wrote but a few sentences ago, is it fortunate to feel oneself aloof? Deep waters here. There is a distinction, a difference in scale, it seems to me, between living a principled life and living a life based upon some profound conviction. But these speculations are always ultimately fruitless. Abstractions are a pitfall I have learned to avoid.

The Challenge of Change: Money Versus People

by Mark William Harrison

The Song of the World

The song of the world is about those who are called unsung.

Who are the unsung?

They are those who are insignificant to the prejudices of money.

In them the waters gather, every drop. In them the question is asked: their voice never wavers.

They are the song, they are the question. They are the answer.

Humans Are Difficult To Subdue

When we are intensely at one with our humanity we are intensely at one with the world, and the expression on our faces is fearless. We feel vibrant, open, radiant: like the wind on the mountains, like the burst of wings. In our essence we are fearless, because in our essence we are the universe.

We are meant to live by truths of the spirit. What are truths of the spirit? They are truths for which there is no visible evidence. Those who look for support in the visible world have become frightened.

When we look directly at another, straight in the eyes, we are asking a question.

What is that question?

What is that question in a society where things are more real than people, and people are always hurrying, and everyone is suspicious of everyone else, and all we ever talk about is money?

The Labyrinth

The mind projects values and principles into the world: the world suggests values and principles to the mind. Mind and world are one: humans inhabit a domain of significance. Failure to establish that domain, a human world, is our only true castastrophe.

In our society that catastrophe has occurred, for the first time on the planet: money values are not human values. Human beings are not wage-earners, a human shelter is not an investment, the Earth is not real estate, knowledge is not property.

How is the world transformed into money?

Whatever can be sold for money is a form assumed by money. If everything in a society—the people, the things people create, the things found in nature—can be bought and sold, then everything has become money. It's that simple. Or, even simpler: if labor is sold, then so will its product.

Thus we are uncertain about what is good or bad, right or wrong, healthy or sick, natural or unnatural, meaningful or meaningless, valuable or worthless. We are uncertain about how our own children should be raised. We are uncertain about what we should eat, how we should make love, why we exist.

Our leaders tell us nothing but the cost.

Voyagers

They stand in line, the inventors of ethics and music, fidgeting with their unemployment booklets. The eyes are keen, the eyes have depth. What quickens in them at each breath, then sinks? They who dreamed, who dared to create: what are they doing here?

When they are young the world is vivid; as they age the world becomes profound. The qualities of a whole planet depend upon them. Through their lips the world sings, through their eyes it sees its infinite beauty; in their minds it knows itself, in their hearts it loves and is loved.

They are distracted on the long lines, nervous and worried, glancing suspiciously at each other. They drag themselves to the glass doors, but a part of them never enters.

They are imagination. They are mathematics. They alone suspected that there is more here than meets the eye. They are language, conscious purpose, the cultivation of plants. They are drama, the intensification of life.

What have they done to themselves?

All We Need Is A Strategy

The eyes of children stare directly at us, watching what we do; they try to figure out the patterns and principles of our behaviour, unaware of the weight of their gaze. The world grows meaningful for the eyes and the mind. Predictability, consistency, relatedness, import and purpose are some of the initial demands we make in the fabrication of a human world.

When we are adults the direct gaze often turns inward, lingering on as a symbol: we stare into space, lost in thought, demanding that the inner world also be human.

The growth of each human is the creation of the world again. We are each a focus, an illumination. The miracle of the universe is the light of consciousness, because only in that light is the universe supported: what we see happening on the faces of children, as they grow, is the re-enactment of creation.

The individual evolution is part of a larger evolution, the evolution of humanity itself. The sense of that evolution is partly veiled, a half-revealed secret, a Mystery. Of one thing, however, we are certain: we can go astray. Love, moral standards and devotion to truth have been our best guides.

In our society, the custodians of the evolution are politicians, executives and generals. Specialists in expediency, finance and violence.

A Lot Goes On Beneath The Surface

"Another day, another dollar!"

What's in the tone of voice there?

It's a sort of bright cheerful resignation, tinged with just the faintest suggestion of bitterness. On a rough day there's an edge of challenge to it, almost belligerence. It's ironic, it's worldly. The acceptance of an insult so massive and familiar and inherent that protest would seem absurd: like protesting heat waves or aging. This is life, that's all there is to it, this is reality. We're in it together. No way out.

The protest, however, does exist: right there in the tone of voice. What it really says is: I'm ready whenever you are.

Unity

We comfort others in the knowledge that comfort cannot be given: we are a harbor where the soul may rest in its pain, we provide the haven where grief may be devoted to itself without having to bother with the details of life. The comforter's eyes and thoughts are calm and detached, withholding the secret, while the sufferer mistakes the sanctuary for the consolation. The burden of carrying on has temporarily been removed, that's all; even the simplest things will be done by someone else for awhile. What we require is a full experience of the sorrow, without distractions.

The deeper knowledge here is the knowledge that life must go on, that we must be equal to its trials. Comforting also has a cold realism it it, a practical function. We provide respite to each other because we have a collective commitment to the value of the endeavor itself: we must be equal to all this because it has a meaning, it contains our own truth within it: denial of the given path is denial of ourselves. What has been given must be accepted, not passively but as the terrain upon which we struggle toward our destiny. When we say "That's life" it is not with resignation, but in the spirit of accepting the terms. So, for everyone's sake, a hand darts out to the one who stumbles.

Now in these dark times we are deeply troubled. Comfort will be demanded and provided, in myriad forms. Each form, degraded or sublime, expresses the one relationship, the one dignity, the one great faith by which the whole world is illuminated and sustained.

The Accumulation Of Capital

The salesman has to make himself appear happy in order to sell successfully. If he weakens or rebels in the face of this demand, he feels that he's betraying his children. The fundamental responsibility, whose denial is spiritual suicide, keeps him in his place. He sticks with it. Silently screaming, going mad in his mind, he sticks with it.

The force or agency which compels the salesman to play this role is clearly hostile to his humanity. On the other hand, and just as clearly, it comprehends the basic truth about his relationship to others in the pursuit of his livelihood: he will not sell if he appears troubled or detached.

This force or agency moves everywhere through our society, we all experience it, and yet there's nobody here but us.

This is the mystery Marx unraveled.

The Actor And The Witness

Sometimes we are one with the action, absorbed. Sometimes we are aware of ourselves, detached, assessing through narrowed eyes.

Who is the actor when we are detached? Where is the witness when we are absorbed?

The actor and the witness are the one humanity, in different states. In one identity we fashion ourselves, in the other we examine our work, and speculate.

The actor is becoming a robot.
The witness's heart is pounding.

A Moment Of Weakness Now And Then Is Also Human

It's the promise, the promise unfulfilled, that tears at the heart. To remember them when they were nothing but the promise, and then to see what becomes of them when they grow up . . .

But this is weakness. To lament that things are not as they should be is to indulge in paralysis. Sometimes it's healthy to recall the hardheadedness of Lenin. The recognition of truth is not where our devotion ends: it's where it begins.

We don't love the ocean less because it's polluted, anymore than we love people less because they're crippled or diseased. Love perceives the wholeness, always: the essence. Whatever is damaged, whatever needs to be healed, is asking for love.

Insurgence reveals its meaning to the love of life, as the meaning of water is revealed to thirst.

Insurgence Is Being In Tune With Things

We feel hope when we see expressions of genuine concern. Concern for life, concern for others, concern for values, concern for the future, concern for whatever is precious. Concern is demanded of us.

Concern implies a belief that things ought to be a certain way, or go in a certain direction: it assumes that the world has a meaning, an intention, that everything contains and deserves its appropriate fulfillment.

Concern implies sympathy and empathy: it assumes that beneath the visible separateness there is an invisible continuity and unity—beneath the all is the one.

Concern then is in the nature of things. It's already there. If concern is not expressed, life will seem unreal.

Strength

A fifteen-year-old girl was raped and her arms hacked off just below the elbows. How are we supposed to go on being human where this has happened? This and all the other things.

The answer is a paradox:

We overcome despair and madness by embracing the very reality which urges us to these defeats. This is the insurgent's method. We embrace it with our hearts, in solidarity with life, with human evolution. The wisdom here is ancient: whatever the heart embraces becomes a source of strength.

Embracing reality means expanding into the experience of others until we realize that there are no others: that we are all one. Pain by pain, grief by grief, walk toward and through the blinding light. Understand laughter; understand remorse; understand fear; understand pride, hatred, envy, irony, dignity. Everything. Understand everything human.

The face of the girl who was raped and mutilated is the face of your daughter. What you summon up when you look at that face is the strength that has sustained us through it all. We endure. We fall apart and then pull ourselves together. We wait till the time is ripe.

The Force Of Life

When a weed manages to poke through the crack where the sidewalk meets a brick wall at right angles it always seems a metaphor for a quality of life, the insurgent quality. We identify with the weed. It's a victory.

We see victory, we see defeat. But the force of life knows only itself: wherever it is, it is complete. Being complete, it is at peace.

We are not at peace. Our hearts are torn. We're beginning to see strange faces when we look in the mirror. Our children use the word "weird" more and more. Who among us doesn't feel that everything is falling apart?

But the force of life is at peace, complete, insurgent.

The Record

We rarely notice immediately that someone's eyes are sad. The dignity is visible first; after that, the sorrow. The face changes in our minds.

The quality of past life imprints itself on the human face. Day by day, year by year, through the deepening seasons and the long bright pain of ripening, our life becomes the face's seams and furrows, the look in the eyes, the nearly invisible shadow at the corner of the mouth. It becomes the movement of the features, quick or deliberate, the lifting of the eyebrows, the way the gaze returns from reverie to respond to a question; it becomes the tone of voice, it becomes posture and gesture. The face and manner record the life, in a language that can only be read by other humans.

So it follows that just as we can learn something about the past from the faces of the elders among us, we can learn something about the present by becoming conscious of our own organic experience: by integrating the organic identity into our lives. The body is never distracted and never deceived. It sees, and becomes, the truth. In becoming whole we discover the truth.

The mind that inscribes our lives on our faces is the mind of the Earth. The scarred Earth, the good Earth, the Blessing.

It drifts, blue and green and white, through the stars and silence of infinite space, inexpressibly beautiful, inexpressible in its loveliness, sacred for eternity, trailing behind it, like grasses in water, its memory, the divine birth of life.

What our children read on our faces they will inherit.

Forms Of Freedom

We can't be serious about anything unless we are free. Freedom has no meaning, however, unless we are serious. Therefore freedom and seriousness go together, each grows out of the other. Their unity is one of the revelations of the human spirit.

This is a society in which some people joke about the end of the world—"Live it up while you can, folks!"—and others chain themselves to redwood trees.

Everybody knows what's going on. We even remind each other from time to time, just to make sure no one can pretend they haven't heard about it.

We Inherit Human Expectations

Often the only reason we can give for a decision is "What else was there to do?" We ask the question with resignation—or bewilderment, or anger, or irony, or desperation: the tone varies, depending on the circumstances and on our individual styles. Sometimes we project a facade of calm rationality, as if the decision, although apparently forced, was made in a state of scientific detachment, the victory of a mature mind: we salvage our dignity.

The tone of voice of the question "What else was there to do?" echoes the mood we were in when we made the decision. That mood may linger beneath the surface for years—faint but pervasive, sometimes smoldering, ready to flare up, sometimes just a dull private pain of regret, one of those sensitive places in the soul—defining a fairly long period of our lives. We enlisted. We got married. We took a job.

It's a matter of the quality of life. It's a matter of pride and self-respect. Playing the roles offered to us by this society, we have a sense of being used.

Banking

The checkbook evokes a special seriousness, almost solemnity. We handle it with respect. We scrutinize the computations through narrowed eyes. We review the entries, our brows furrowed, trying to ferret out mistakes, reliving the taut decisions. Sometimes we just stare at the figures. There's always a faint halo of tension around a checkbook; terrible things can happen here.

In a sequence of numerals, linked by strict addition and subtraction, the checkbook reels off a diary in arithmetic: the latest balance, a very important number, is a description of our lives at that moment. It may be alarming or consoling; it may even be incorrect. Here is the career of the financial identity: our true biography, as far as Capital is concerned: the actual person. In that biography, the form assumed by hopes, plans, dreams and needs, responsibility, generosity and happiness—the human modes of being—is money. These human modes of being can accumulate interest, draw dividends, be loaned or taxed, mortgaged or invested, deposited or withdrawn. They all look the same.

The power that transforms our lives into money is lethal. The whales and redwoods, for example, were gone before the harpoon struck or the axe fell, from the moment they became money. The same with all the fur, plumes, hides, shells, flesh and fiber, the hardwoods and the habitats. The same with ideas, memories, history, childcare, healing, silence and peace of mind. Capital looked their way, they became dollars and cents.

Whatever becomes money disappears in that moment: whatever is loved becomes real. Love creates reality. All beings await the vision that loves, because only in that vision are they born: only in that vision can they flourish and rejoice in themselves and each other.

Whenever we talk about our lives in the language of money, it's really money talking about us.

Facing Reality

If we lost a child, and were equal to it, a Presence would be revealed that would live with us for the rest of our lives, and be our strength. By that Presence we would know the truth of every moment. We would know what is precious and what is necessary, we would discover patience and eternity, we would be rescued from depravity; we would fulfill our responsibilities without fail. The one Life that is in all would become visible to us, and we would realize that we have never loved anything but that one Life, and that whatever loves or is loved is that one Life. The inner eye that sees the radiance would be opened, bringing peace. What needs to be done would be done.

The condition of humanity in these times, if we can face it, establishes that same Presence among us. As with the death of the child, all we have to do is face reality.

Correct Ideas Don't Drop From The Sky: They Come From The Heart

Many people no longer kill anything. People who used to step on ants or worms or snails now walk around them. Even the tiniest murders are beginning to seem violent; they summon up images: hydrogen bombs, stupendous continuous explosions, chunks of earth and shattered bodies hurtled spraying in slow motion through darkened air, filling the whole sky: megatons of ordnance. There's been enough death, quite enough death. We stare at insects as if seeing them for the first time, watching how they move. Little living things.

Regard all life as sacred: this is the ancient law. When we are aware of it, it is obeyed: when it is not obeyed, we become aware of it. All the real laws operate like that. The universe issues warnings before it delivers the sentence.

The universe is Spirit. The laws are spiritual. The warnings are spiritual events. We can hear them because we are capable of oneness with Spirit—the primal staggering truth about human beings. We can hear them, and we can ignore them. They tell us what is at stake.

We Never Feel Joy On Smoggy Days

The cells of the body try to reject the smog. We experience this attempt to repel the poisons as a flutter of panic, an impulse to flight. We are cranky, tense, quick to argue. Strange lightnings flare through the brain, almost too brief to record, interrupting the stream of thought.

The cells remember pure air, the blue crystal bell of the sky, the music of breezes. They remember the clear delicious waters, the cool green intoxicating odor of the grass. The cells were at one with the world, they loved it. Their rejection of the smog is proof of their memory. The cells know the way things should be on the Earth.

A warning like the one we receive from the cells cannot be ignored. And we are receiving other warnings just like it, all the time, from other guardian angels, faithful hearts within us.

Where The Stock Market Crashed

We inform ourselves about the busy affairs of money. How much, where it is going, the rise and fall of prices, the budget; taxes, wages, interest, investment, profit and loss. There's a whole world in which the characters are money in its many forms. All our relationships to each other, as social beings, take place in that feverish unpredictable invisible world. We observe it nervously; we're given reports about it, twenty-four hours around the clock.

This is what Marx meant when he said that Capital is a social relationship. This is the real insight. We are people who carry our relationships to others in our pockets, deposit them in banks, receive them in the mail, transport them in armored cars, store them away in computers in the form of digital impulses. The world of money, obeying the laws of money, is our world. It exists between all of us, but not within us. Individually, in our essence, we are humanity: collectively, in our society, we have become Capital.

So we carry on, under these strange circumstances: as a matter of fact, these are the very circumstances we continually refer to when we say "We're doing our best under the circumstances." Two worlds which are yet one. What happens in the world of money happens in our lives.

For example, there was nothing unusual in the world of life on the night of October 24th, 1929. Some slept soundly, others wakened fitfully, some dreamt about childhood friends. Some made love late into the night, some wished they'd had the strength. Mothers got up at four a.m. to nurse the baby; children kicked their blankets off and were covered again. In the kitchens the dinner dishes dried, the hearth fires sank to embers. People smoked cigarettes in dark silent rooms, or plucked aimlessly on guitar strings; some leaned on the window sill to stare thoughtfully one last time at the bare autumn branches etched against the fading sky, before they sighed and climbed the stairs with a heavy tread. The infinite life of the Earth quietly celebrated, as always, its immemorial harmony. The relationships of the day just ended hung suspended, like smoke, defining the terrain of fears and hopes for the day about to dawn.

But that night, while everyone slept, the stock market crashed and the Great Depression began: eleven years long till we entered the War and finally got the economy back on its feet again.

Through Wage Labor People Become Capital . . . But Never Completely

Think of this:

The elders among us are maintained just a hair—a penny would be more apt: we are referring here to a calculation—

above the level where their visible abandonment and degradation would cause public dismay. They crumple just after
they've closed the door behind them; the shameful testimony has always just been snatched out of sight. There is a
satanic intimacy in our very midst.

Now think of this:

When we see the slightly damaged humans among us,
those called retarded—playing awkwardly and excitedly in
the parks, showing childlike vexation on their faces when
their aides urge them along, smiling shyly or not at all when
we catch their eyes—we feel the presence of humanity very
intensely. We see the tiny but incredibly crucial gap, the
exquisite delicacy of the human balance. A nerve, a milli-
gram. These also are maintained among us, like the elders.
The resources are available and allocated.

Money has to reckon with people.

The Flower And The Soil

From the beginning we realized that the ability to perceive
ourselves from without was essential to our preservation
and evolution: we are the being which creates its identity: in
us the universal creativity has achieved consciousness: we
participate, but not yet totally, in the divine.

Therefore we discovered or invented places where we
could stand and observe ourselves, interpret our situation
and behavior, discriminate between conformity and
deviance, between development and regression. We speculated, debated, experimented, fabricated and recorded; we
learned to present ourselves to ourselves for contemplation,
in theater, ceremony, art, symbol.

In those places of detachment, if we were successful, we
identified ourselves first with the unchanging truths, the
guiding values and ideals we had created as intrinsic to our
humanity—sincerity, generosity, compassion, courage,
responsibility, respect: the virtues—and second with the

sense of the dynamic, with the indestructible intuition of our evolution toward a destiny which cannot be named or known, only lived. At our best we gave ourselves the great answers, the religions: illumination, salvation and peace.

Cosmos and history, the Earth and its people. We know we are involved in an infinite miracle: incredible as it seems, we may actually be on the threshold of deciphering the purpose of an infinite Spirit. We are drama: excitement beyond measure.

On this level, the level of destiny, we are now imperiled.

But there's another level of our humanity, another drama: ordinary daily life. We struggle against ourselves, against our waywardness and wilfullness, our foolishness and self-ishness, our foibles and shallow self-deceptions, our apparently inveterate tendency to forget the covenant when we think we can get away with it. We are a mixture of silliness and nobility, of weakness and goodness; we fall short of our own honest ideals, and our attempts to live up to them, especially as we recount them afterwards, are quite often hilarious. We are amused by ourselves, patient with ourselves, firm but also indulgent, because we love and understand ourselves. After all, we're only human.

We sneak, we plead, we fake, we gamble; we're crafty, reckless and ridiculous; we imitate dignity when we're caught red-handed. We snivel, bluster and pout. Our schemes backfire on us and then we lie about them and everybody knows we're lying. We are funny. We often describe our behavior—something that happened, something someone did—as very human. This is recognition of our earthiness.

We are the soil of ourselves: good rich soil. The laughter and the juices, the zest and the backbone. The grumbling stubborn faith. The wicked gleam in the eye.

It's odd, but on this level it seems we are immortal.

The Ecosphere

Loneliness is life starved for life. Its pain increases as the level of life sinks and access to life diminishes. Widespread loneliness is a warning that the ecosystem is dying, that the level of life is falling dangerously low. Loneliness, in other words, is a condition of the Earth: the Earth's experience of the pain of dying. Its opposite is the joy of growing.

The suffering of loneliness is very great, sometimes unendurable. We panic, huddling into ourselves in fear of death; we writhe and wail, we become frenzied; we subside into whimpers, the whole world reduced to a soundless, utterly indifferent desolation. We drink, we become eccentric, we go mad, we jump from bridges, we giggle hysterically. We become the weird people in the neighborhood, never seen without a dog, always wearing the same clothing, wary and secretive out of a terrible vulnerability. Some of us live out an entire lifetime in loneliness, saved only by responsibility, or consciousness of dignity, or the simple stubborn tenacity of life.

When the immigrants arrived in this country, uprooted, compelled by remote inscrutable decisions to leave the world of life—soil and stock, seasons and weathers, the feel of sun and rain—for the world of money—factories, machinery and stifling tenements, the stupendous dynamo of industrial capitalism—the one thing they knew for certain was that they were lonely.

Body And Soul

On the surface we have feelings: anger, bitterness, exhaustion, disgust. At the core we have knowledge: that this life is unworthy of us.

The feelings are responses of our organic being. The attribute of the organic being is zest; zest is the active creative love of life; the organic response to Capital is deflected or frustrated zest. Earth. The organic is the Earth.

The knowledge is human self-consciousness: the spirit in history. We know how hard it was, how great we are. Each of us remembers the whole journey, every step of the way. We recognize the slightest insult, instantly. How could it be otherwise? We've been deadly serious about ourselves for a million years.

Look at us! We take our breath away. To think that such a creature as we are should die a death as ignominious as the one we seem to be preparing for ourselves brings tears to our eyes. It can't happen. It just can't happen.

Evolution

We get scared that maybe we're going crazy. This is an error, because it's actually the society which is crazy, not us. The perception is correct, our lives here are truly insane, but we misplace the blame. The human fulfillment in meaning, balance and harmony is coextensive with the universe, so fundamental that its absence drives us to challenge even the integrity of our own souls. Meaninglessness, imbalance and disharmony, however, can be addressed only when they are understood as political problems. We blame ourselves only because we are disorganized.

The response, on its level, is valid.

We become frustrated and furious, mad at our own lives. We do what we're supposed to do and still everything goes wrong, we still get screwed, we're still miserable. So we lash out at whoever is closest; then we suffer remorse. Again the focus is turned inward rather than outward, and for the same reason. Our lives are maddening because we have accepted a bad bargain in good faith. Rage is legitimate in a crooked society.

The response, on its level, is valid.

We feel invisible and conclude in desperation that something is lacking or undeveloped within us. We try to make ourselves interesting or attractive by purchasing accessories eagerly presented to us as exactly what we need. Invariably we are deceived, and this is as intended: our perpetual hopeful return to the marketplace is essential to the circulation of commodities, and the circulation of commodities is what it's all about. Capitalism's blindness to anything human is what makes us feel invisible.

The response, on its level, is valid.

A million years of victory have gone into the fashioning of each one of us. A million trophies hang in every heart. We are the humans.

Money Talks

Money, in the form of advertising jingles, sometimes bounces maddeningly in our brains for weeks. The ingenuity of the composers and performers was purchased with this precise goal in mind. We know what kinds of music will stick in our heads. Through wage labor our own ingenuity is harnessed to the strategies of Capital. This is why the things that are done to us often seem absolutely fiendish.

Whenever we buy something, receive a paycheck, pay a bill, deposit our earnings in a bank, apply for a loan—any of a thousand transactions—it's really money relating to itself: we're merely the agents, the real characters are sums of money. In the millions of forms we fill out, money is ascertaining information about itself. Our daily lives are the pipes through which money circulates. This is why we often feel unreal or dead.

Because money is a relationship between people transformed into a thing, every nickel we have is really a symbol of all we don't have: the infinite richness waiting to spring to life in each face-to-face human encounter. This is why our hearts often feel empty.

We save for a rainy day and invest in our future. When we're healthy we look like a million bucks, when we're sick we get the best doctor money can buy, when we die we cash in our chips. We worry about the cost of living. We pay our own way.

It's everywhere. It's the language of nations, it's war and peace: it's the measure of time and space. How will we break its hold upon us? Where would we begin? Who has any ideas? The asking of these questions was the destiny of protoplasm, all along. The warm ooze that learned to crawl and mate, that became flowers and eagles and laughter.

"That Generations May Not Fail In The Future . . ."
—Hako Ritual, Pawnee

If we knew this was the last generation, if we knew there would be no more children, then we could no longer experience joy.

This is knowledge of the heart, intuitive truth. We can know certain things because we're able to identify with our essence. This particular knowledge teaches us that the experience of joy is based upon confidence in the continuity of generations, in the continuity of life. Because we've always taken that continuity for granted, we were not aware that our joy was based upon it.

But now the thought crosses our minds. A quiet sharp-edged shadow passes over our hearts from time to time. We stare at children with a new intensity. Their innocence seems tragic as well as precious; we look for signs of the latent nobility of the race, knowing that's what the situation will call for. Nobility. Strength.

We've become conscious of what we've been doing to ourselves all these years, behind our own backs. It can't be hidden anymore.

We Take Ourselves Very Seriously

When the widow broke down and cried at the prospect of going through her dead husband's papers to find out exactly how much welfare and social security she was entitled to, the social worker urged her to take a Valium. Factory workers, clerical workers, housewives, managers, teenagers, athletes, students, teachers, marines, doctors, lawyers, teamsters and waitresses all take pills, pills are everywhere.

We have perfected techniques for inducing anesthesia in our souls. It's a two-edged sword, however, because when we numb the pain in our souls we numb the soul itself. We pay that price.

Let's understand it clearly:

In the intention of humanity, anesthesia numbs the pain: the pain of fear, stress, anxiety, despair, loneliness, emptiness, nausea, boredom and so on: the goal is survival. In the intention of Capital, anesthesia numbs the soul: the real effect of all the tranquilizing agents, including television, is stupefaction: the goal is counter-insurgency. Each aims at insuring our continued functioning and nothing more, humanity motivated by self-love, Capital by the need to guarantee the reproduction of tractable labor power. This double intention becomes one through the mysterious alchemy of wage labor: we are humanity in the form of Capital. Such is our situation.

Humanity is a creature self-endowed with personality, imagination, curiosity, ingenuity, sensitivity, memory, discrimination and causal insight, a creature whose essence is creativity, whose sheer superfluous organic exuberance compels it to create even when asleep. We invented murder, slaughter, carnage and war. We're the triumph of a million years of cunning. We're inherently dangerous, treacherous and tenacious: formidable: literally awesome. Our enemies live in fear: they can't turn their backs on us for a second. And where are we going? Our destiny is divine, oneness with that infinite love which is God: the whole universe propels us towards it.

Anesthesia is the master strategy. From both points of view. We increase the dosage every day.

Don't Miss The Double Meaning In The Punch Line!

He pats his wallet pocket and says, with a swagger, "I tell my wife she has nothing to worry about as long as we've got this!"

He's right. In capitalist society money will buy anything: therefore the only thing we have to worry about is running out of money.

In the larger picture, however, where humanity as a whole is concerned, we're in the worst crisis in all history. We face the real possibility of the end of life on Earth.

It seems, then, that capitalist society tends to make people insane, at the same time as it makes perfect sense on its own terms.

Clearly we are capable of diabolical ingenuity, and therefore will be very difficult to defeat.

Seasons

Mortality is the spirit's method on this planet. Birth and death are the organic intervals through which the force of life evolves its ever-changing forms, pursuing the unknowable goal. Perpetual rebirth, therefore, can be considered one of our weapons. We move through a sequence of selves. When we feel our humanity dying in an old self, we abandon it and are reborn in a new one. This is one way of understanding history.

The old self dies because it can't face death. It refuses to face the fact that reality is the scene of its death. Therefore it loses its creativity: its life is pretense and its essence is fear. The new self faces reality it accepts death, dies and is reborn. It is humanity again, its own reality, and therefore fearless. Its essence is creative love, the supreme power of the human race. The only power that can defeat Capital.

Mothers and fathers, sons and daughters, the mortal seed, the immortal spirit. Lenin insisted it could be accomplished

by a vanguard party, Mao proclaimed "Bombard the head-
quarters!" The people working swing shift and graveyard,
their minds a million miles away, slam the forklifts into gear;
teenagers shamble to the fast-food parking lots, passing a
joint. In fleeting moments we catch each other's eyes for an
instant, stare intently, then quickly turn away, feeling
puzzled and thinking wild thoughts.

Some of us announce, with measured emphasis, "I want to
get it all out of my system." Others say, grinning mischie-
vously, "I'm for real!" As we grow older, understanding life
more deeply every year, and our children grow taller, gradually facing and becoming the future, we fall in love with them
over and over again.

Zeroing In

When we ask each other how we're doing these days, we
often answer in terms of survival: "Oh, I guess I'll survive!"
Or, "Just trying to survive, that's all!" Or, simply, "Surviving!" And we accompany the words with a significant glance,
grim determination coupled with helpless amazement at the
madness of everything.

Obviously this is one of those little glimpses into history.
The same fleeting exchange, the same word and glance,
repeated a million times a day.

Survival.

We'll have to learn how to speak from the heart again.
How to trust each other. How to recognize a failure of nerve.

Survival.

The plow, the loom, the potter's wheel and the sailboat.
The barrel, the windlass, the wagon and the lathe, the hoe
and the broom, the axe and the net, the water-wheel, the
harness and the cradle. Simple and brilliant. Our favorite
style.

Survival.

Gas a dollar a gallon. Rents unbelieveable. Even with

husband and wife both working we can barely make it.

Most of us just live from day to day, hoping our leaders will somehow bring us safely through the crisis, although we don't have much confidence in them, and we're slowly losing the ability to care about it all. The teenagers smoke dope and listen to amplified rock; the students, we are told, have become conservative The socialists, in dwindling numbers, still plug away in the crevices conceded to them by the ruling class. The remnants of the black, feminist and hippie militants, hardly even pausing for nostalgia, have redefined their lives. The trade union movement is just another computerized bureaucracy, contesting distribution of the surplus. Some people say the nuclear power and weapons protest has the potential to become a national movement. That would be promising, because the issue is life itself. The real issue.

Survival.

After the sun has set behind the ridge, a few hills on the coastal range still catch the strong warm yellow glow. On the other side, invisible, the Pacific is shimmering like a trillion jewels. We trudge back, thinking with the Earth.

Night. The star-studded heavens, infinity of stars, the brain of God. Dark surf breaking on the dark beach. The murmuring Earth, realm of life, source of music. The humans, dreaming.

The Singer And The Song

We hear the praise of the world within us, the celebration of existence, like a song always being sung, a song which is actually our own true voice. When we sing the song we become one with it: when we become one with it we become one with the universe: the singing fills everything that exists. We know then that the whole world is a celebration, that the entire universe, in every atom and every instant, is the praise of God. We ascend into the unutterable bliss:

absolute freedom and peace, infinite humility: That I should
be a portion of such glory! The ego disappears. We enter the
divine Oneness.

This experience is attested and recorded among all peo-
ples. The memory of it, the techniques for attaining it—
yogic meditation, fasting in the wilderness, drugs, chanting
and dancing, ecstatic trance, ascetic discipline, ritual orgy, a
life of universal compassion, entry into the Void or the Tao
or the Brahman, adoration of Mary, Jesus or the Saints: the
variety itself is a miracle—are preserved and transmitted
from generation to generation. The pursuit of transcendence is constant and central in the human legacy.

The praise of the world is like a song within us and within
all things. There's nothing uglier than the noise with which
we drown it out, and nothing more beautiful than the way
we can sing it when we really try. That's because we're the
only ones who sing it so we can hear it. The ocean sings it,
the land sings it, everything alive sings the song. But we're
the only ones who sing it because we love to hear it, and
because we know it's the right thing to do, and because we
want to be accepted.

Worrying And Solidarity

In capitalist society, the form assumed by communal life is
buying and selling: the existence of the community is purchased. Food, clothing and shelter, excitement, information,
inspiration, reassurance and instruction, musicians, healers
and leaders, heat and light, assistance of all kinds, instruments of communication—all are bought and sold.

The amount of community we can purchase depends
upon how much money we have. Because that amount is
determined by inhuman considerations, remote or unjust,
we worry a lot.

When we worry about money we lie awake at night, our
minds tilted from fatigue, trying to think of schemes,

reviewing the same dubious alternatives over and over again hoping they'll reveal some new angle; we quarrel over nickels and dimes, accusing each other of irresponsibility or stupidity or deliberate sabotage; every need or preference, every plan or suggestion, the sight of the children or the car or a crack in the plaster, reminds us suddenly of money, income is not keeping pace with expenses. We harbor a terrified anticipation of public shame.

Money troubles make us aware of how alone we all are: aware that the money community possesses no more human content than a chunk of ice adrift in space, and is as utterly indifferent to the spectacle of human need as the eye of a dead fish. We have friends, of course. They lend us money. Good friends lend us money no questions asked. They say "Pay me back wherever you can, don't worry about it."

The Basic Lesson Of Capitalist Society

We tell them: "You're going to have to learn the value of money!" It comes across as a warning. Our voices are harsh. Are we talking about responsibility or surrender?

We're talking about both, and the warning tone is appropriate. We want them to survive, meaning get serious about money: Capital wants them to submit, meaning the same thing.

So we pounce on them, exasperated and fed up, and they bluster and mutter sullen excuses; we watch carefully for the precise moment to end the harangue and begin the advice, and they toy with silverware, every now and then suddenly meeting us eye to eye to see if we'll look away. A thousand nuances in ten minutes flat.

Capital and humanity, center stage, command performance.

Point Of View

Our hands enjoy the textures and contours of natural things, and of things made by hand. They feel confident with them. Shells and stones, bark and hair, woven baskets, carved handles, manila rope, radishes, bananas and woolen blankets, bamboo flutes, leather and bread. Anything made of wood. Things like these are familiar to the skin, understandable, predictable. Everything we discover about them confirms an intuition our hands already contained. The explanation, whether we consult chemistry, ecology, biology or religion, is clear: one source, one substance.

In this society, the world our hands inhabit is almost entirely standardized, mass-produced and dead. There's very little actual skin contact with anything in its original state: lots of boxes, packages and cans, switches, buttons and knobs. Styrofoam cups and ball-point pens. Almost everything our hands touch is either metal or processed or some kind of synthetic, usually a petroleum derivative. Often they repeat the same cramped mindless motions all day long, like machines: sorting screws, making change, stacking cartons, filing receipts, drilling holes, typing letters. What happens to them in this world?

They become bored. Never ignorant—everything is ultimately of the Earth, even plastic has learnable tactile patterns—and always curious at first, because that's their nature, but always finally bored: they become competent, a little brutal and bored. Analogies are numerous and obvious.

Hands. They feel at their best with musical instruments, faithful well-made tools, sports equipment, gardens, children, lovers and water. They scratch where we itch and rub where we hurt. They live in the world they fashion, our whole world, blind.

We Ourselves Are The Victory

The love of life itself is felt as delight. When we catch a glimpse of the life in people, the life itself as a pure essence, we feel a leap of delight. The love comes first, unveiling the essence, and then the sight of the essence ignites delight in the heart of the love, like a spark.

Spiritual reality is infinite delight. This sequence describes one of our methods of entry into that reality. The conclusions we draw after we return—and we always return, because our drama and our task are here—guide us in the conduct of daily life.

We begin to free ourselves from Capital by becoming conscious of human styles and methods. We think them through, we describe, analyze and interpret them. It's not only a response to servitude: this is the way we always did it, this is our specific technique. Nothing is more familiar to us, nothing more exciting. The voice that asks the question "Who am I?" is the voice that knows the answer.

The Retirement Years

When the woman in her eighties unexpectedly declared to someone half her age—not exactly with gladness but with a kind of solemn conviction, like a profession of faith—"It's a beautiful day!" he immediately had a revelation of the Earth as the realm of life: the place where we are alive, the only place we'll ever be alive, our one chance: every moment infinitely precious. In the sound of her voice, the routine details of the urban scene withdraw into themselves like worshippers lowering their eyes before the passing of a holy image, acknowledging the arrival of the grandeur that sustains and contains them: the living Earth. The beautiful days remaining to her are numbered. Illuminated by her mortality, they became for him what they really are, sacred not only in themselves, but above all for what they reveal beyond them. This entire drama occurred in the human soul, the one soul in both of them, and in all of us.

We cannot unveil a certain deep reality of things by our own effort. It requires the actual presence of old people. We don't see very much of old people, however. Because Capital can no longer extract surplus value from their labor, they have no role in the society; they become invisible.

The enrichment old people can donate to our lives has all but disappeared from our experience: to that degree we are diminished, held back from entering the infinite miracle our creativity discovers. They're afraid to walk outdoors now, because teenagers might attack them. There are articles in the papers every day about how they're beaten, raped and murdered. The teenagers, of course, are not to blame: they're only products of capitalist society, the society which has nothing human to teach them and awaits only their maturation into labor power; till then they can roam the streets. In nursing homes old human beings are drugged, propped up in front of television sets and left there, fretting and drooling, all day long. Many of them eat dog food. From the point of view of Capital they're just a drain on the investment process.

Hatred of the ruling class is a healthy invigorating feeling. It sends a joyful smile to our faces and kindles a radiance in our eyes: our hearts exult. Class War is a phrase that has been translated into every language on Earth.

Myth And Reality

Our most common image of paradise is a celestial Earth. Sunshine, rivers and the song of birds, purity, harmony and peace. Robed figures with serene smiles seated beneath blooming trees in postures of repose. Timelessness. The heavenly afterlife is a divine Earth. We long for a static bliss, the unity of spiritual oneness and earthly delight.

The image of a terrestrial paradise can only have originated in the accumulation of living memories; the cultural symbol emerges from actual experience, from the glimpses we are granted. This experience, however, is generated by the spiritual force moving through the universe. The will to immortality and the will to fulfill our essence are the same will: we are of one essence with the Earth: therefore we become immortal on an Earth become divine. Which is another way of saying we become ourselves on an Earth that is loved. It all hangs together.

It all hangs together, and yet there's still something disturbing about it. We're a restless kind of creature. We tend to look for trouble.

Responsibility

The Earth has lost something of its former glory.

This truth is received by human beings in the manner of someone learning of a great personal calamity, like the death of their entire family. First it's unacceptable. We close our eyes, our faces contorted with grief, and shake our heads rhythmically or violently from side to side, wailing "No, no, no, it's not true, I don't believe it!" Then disintegration: we drift through a blurred interim of delirium in which we no longer exist as a coherent personality: nothing is left but the fragments of a shattered world. We lose all sense of time; afterwards we barely remember it. In the last stage we emerge from the chaos into the stillness: gradually, painfully, we begin to identify with what is left of us: the core, the path, the purpose. We resolve to go on living, because healing is one of the great realities, and for the sake of life itself. This is how we receive the great truth about the planet.

The Earth has lost something of its former glory.

The loss occurs only in human experience, because only in human experience does the glory exist in the first place: it shines for us alone. Only humans lose the shore birds, the rivers and the wilderness, the majesty of the endless terrain. The glory of Creation is our offering to the Spirit in return for the Spirit's gift within us, which is, of course, nothing other than the power that creates, sustains and adores that glory: Spirit Itself. The Earth's loss of glory, in other words, is the dying of spiritual power in humanity.

The Earth has lost something of its former glory.

Maybe a voice heard in a dream: the opening sentence of an address to the entire planet, delivered by heroes and heroines of the revolution on the morning after total victory. They stand, looking out over the jubilant crowds, their faces radiant, on a platform in Hiroshima, in the midst of garlands, music and children. If it takes ten thousand years, they declare, we'll devote ourselves to restoring the life we've destroyed. We'll build a new world, where everyone will grow into the true self, the self that says, smiling with bliss, "The love of Thy Creation is what I am!" Dreams are peculiar: they're childish, yet they well up from the depths.

The Earth has lost something of its former glory.

The oceans are almost dead. The large mammals are all but extinct. Nearly all the habitats are wiped out. Concrete, garbage and machinery have penetrated almost everywhere. There's poison in the mother's milk. No words can describe the scale of the catastrophe, no mind can contain it; compared with what there used to be, there's very little left.

The Earth has lost something of its former glory.

Centuries from now, parents will say to their children: For awhile we were the disgrace of the universe. The way some of us see it today is that we had to learn all there was to know about death before we could love life the way we do now. That's when our great love of life was born, you know. Back then, in the Time of Darkness.

What More Can We Ask?

We watch the silhouette and lineaments of the grown man, the grown woman, taking shape on those who were our children. The muscles and beard, the breasts and hips, casual postures, the hardening, alertness and control, the expanding privacy protected behind the eyes. Biology; nothing new. Nor is it anything new that adolescence focuses our commitment to the future: this is immemorial, as ancient as that dawn when we first surmised or decided we had a purpose to fulfill.

What's new is that they're going to be reduced to a commodity, labor power, they're going to have to sell themselves: reality in the twentieth century is Capital. They're going to become part of a global death machine. For awhile we'll be in it together, then they're on their own.

They'll be the usual assortment of geniuses, numbskulls, hotheads and frauds, born leaders and born fools, bunglers, fanatics, vagabonds, parasites and screwballs, cowards, thinkers, singers, saints, heroes, heroines and clowns, fighters and loners, schemers and worriers, traitors, daredevils, visionaries and fiends, the whole cast of characters. That great incredible humanity we love so very much. The people who got us this far.

Habitat

Boredom is the pain we feel when we're not on human terrain. Human terrain is where we grow. Where our potentials are challenged and nourished, where we gladly give and receive ourselves, where necessity and responsibility are one. Human terrain is where we discover and create our humanity. We're intrigued by it, we recognize ourselves there, we become confident and impassioned.

In capitalist society boredom is inherent. Work is boring because it's just a thing we do to earn a wage, beyond that it has no meaning for us. It becomes more boring with every year, for the following reason: The goal of the whole system is the accumulation of capital, the accumulation of capital depends upon the production of surplus value, the production of surplus value increases with the productivity of labor, and the productivity of labor increases, as Capital discovered long ago, when each person performs one mindless mechanical function over and over again. What is perpetually instituted by Capital in the name of greater efficiency is experienced by humans as boredom approaching hysteria.

On the job, therefore, the content of our lives shrivels to the absolute minimum short of coma: obsession with the passage of time. Off the job, we are left to figure out what to do with ourselves in the world we created while we were bored to death. Capital is the invasion and occupation of human terrain.

People who are bored tend to become destructive: boredom, however, is a sign that destruction has already begun. The commonwealth is being dismantled. This whole society, in its imagery and its reality, is gradually becoming a continuous revelation of imperiled life. We are fascinated by violence and disaster; destruction seems both natural and inevitable. The thing we do most often when we are bored is turn on the television set: the facial expressions we see there, if we can see them through human eyes, are either blank or savage.

Reassurance

Every now and then our minds suddenly flash inward to calm a flutter of hysteria. We concentrate, draw a deep breath, maybe shudder, it passes, and we carry on. This happens to all of us: at work and on the freeway, alone or in the midst of friends, even while we're eating. Ripples of terror or anguish: they come and they go.

There's a religious explanation which would go something

like this:

Human evolution is dynamic Spirit, the infinite force which continuously becomes the universe: its intentions are our creativity, its holiness is our destiny. It is equally the organic self and the immortal soul, the imagination and the practiced hand. It is even our freedom to deviate from its truth and the warning that we have done so. In this interpretation, hysteria, like anxiety or remorse, is such a warning: divine intention and human creativity no longer coincide. Spirit is everything: when our feet leave the path of spiritual growth they land on the path of spiritual pain.

There's also a political explanation:

Our lives in this society are shaped by Capital's hunger to accumulate rather than humanity's memory of its truths and exploration of its potentials. The rate of accumulation approaches a maximum as the whole society becomes more and more like a machine. Since money and mechanism are indifferent to life, human or non-human, the expansion of their dominion—money as decision, mechanism as instrument—brings death. Hysteria, in this interpretation, like dread or revulsion, is our reaction to enforced participation in dehumanization and death. It's the voice of human protest within us gradually, in disbelief and horror, losing hope of being answered, or recognized, or even heard.

Finally, there's an ecological explanation which would point out that hysteria is simply our knowledge that we have separated ourselves from the primal source of peace.

All three explanations are true. They clarify why we drink to numb our nerves, mutter or scream in private, tremble when the alarm goes off, pray fervently before the bathroom mirror, and fight our way into a state of mind called madness.

In each life the entire drama unfolds. Our task is to find one another, and prevail together.

Economics

The great theme, constant through it all, is the confrontation between humanity and Capital. There are always only two characters on the stage.

What is Capital?

Capital is the name we give to the social relationship in which humanity has become wage labor. Or, put another way, when human beings are laboring for wages, purchased and doing the job they were paid to do, they become Capital. Finally, Capital can also be understood as the social system generated by money striving to create more of itself, and as that particular kind of money.

Human beings in this system are first of all a commodity: they're bought and sold in a job market. They are a unique commodity, however, in that they can produce wealth, and under the proper conditions more wealth than the cost of their maintenance: a surplus. Since the accumulation of capital, *for its own sake*, is both the driving force and the goal of the whole system, our labor power is purchased and set in motion, or capital is invested, only in order to produce that surplus wealth: only where profit can be made, there and no place else: it makes no difference what we do or make or leave undone, how we feel or what we think. Therefore, as Capital, we create a society devoid of human intention or meaning: human evolution, the self-creation of humanity, goes mad, because the decisions which direct our creativity are made by money. Those who are most willing and able to obey the laws of money, and those who inherit it, their sons, become men of power and influence: our leaders. They compose a social class: the ruling class. Humanity's role, the creation of more money, is called work.

We became wage labor with the formation of capitalist society, when we lost the land and all we had and there was nothing left to do but emigrate to the cities and sell ourselves. Either factories, squalor and disease, or beggary, prison and death: as always, we chose life. Now, in the new system, we are called workers, we're supposed to love money and the things money can buy, and we're supposed to believe that price is the measure of worth—for everything, even human beings.

And that's about it, the essence of it anyway. It's truly cosmic. The universe is Spirit moving toward Itself: the human essence, evolving through self-discovery and self-creation, is part of that movement: as Capital, we betray ourselves, the universe and God. Capital, in other words, is Hell.

Monday through Friday we get up in the morning and go to work. Fight the rush hour traffic both ways. Television in the evening. Saturday and Sunday we recuperate. Then back again on Monday. At regular intervals, a day called payday. Two weeks vacation a year; after five years, three. Until we die or retire. We call it "the grind" and "the rat race," we call ourselves "cogs in the machine," we say "TGIF." At the same time we take pride in our work and try to do a good job: self-respect is one of our attributes. We admire thoroughness, skill, mastery of the task. No one wants to be called a bad worker.

Capital is the combined strength of all of us confronting the separate strength of each of us. That's why its power seems so overwhelming, its ingenuity so devastating. The last words of a martyr are usually worth thinking about. Joe Hill's were: "Don't mourn—organize."

We Are What We Love

We love to hear stories—or play cards or go to the movies or visit with friends—because we love human nature in action: characters and motivations, the unwinding of the plot, the way life keeps the faith, answering every challenge with a lesson. We love humanity as a story.

We love beach-combing, gathering shells and inspecting

sea-things washed up on the beach, because it's an escape into the eternal present, the aboriginal freshness of time we long to recapture, every moment shining like the first, fascinating, delicious, pregnant with amazing discoveries.

We love singing and dancing, because they bring us into harmony with the most obvious sublimity of the universe: joyous beautiful self-expression.

We love eating, sleeping and orgasm, for the same reason animals love eating, sleeping and orgasm: because the force which became life revels in its triumph: it gloats over every idea that worked.

We love the Earth by identity. The rich potentials of the earthly setting, born in the human imagination, are brought to fulfillment by the human creativity they stimulate, establishing a new setting and the start of another cycle: since imagination and creativity are themselves a part of the earthly setting, human evolution is the Earth's growing awareness of itself, its perception, realization and celebration of its own potentials. Therefore our love of the Earth is the Earth's love of humanity.

We love the preservation of human evidence, the mystery of human existence and the truth beneath the surface of events, because we grow by understanding ourselves, by deciphering, remembering, interpreting, probing.

We love those who live a consecrated life—the courage, sacrifice and greatness of soul, the fidelity to principle, the obedience before invisible realities—because they prove we can rise above the emptiness that haunts us.

We love this kind of knowledge, this kind of thinking, for its own sake, because it validates our intuition of cosmic coherence.

And who are we, we who love all these things?

When we look at the faces of sleeping children we feel a great tenderness. When we look at the faces of sleeping adults we feel a great respect. The first is recognition of what is precious: the second is recognition of mortality. Like all living creatures, we know who we are because we recognize ourselves.

Escape

Things pile up and the feeling of being trapped in our own lives becomes so sickening that our nervous systems scream for the instant release of explosive flight: just get up and cut out, get the hell out of here, disappear forever and start fresh all over again someplace else. Any halfway measure would just add to the complexity of the trap.

Escape. We always dream about escape. How could it be otherwise? Think of who we are: it's obvious that we don't belong here. We are the pursuit of significance. We are wonder and curiosity. We are the hunger for the sacred. We are responsibility and coherence, trustworthiness and restraint, dignity, integrity and compassion. We are sympathy and empathy, authenticity and sincerity, kindness and endurance, forgiveness, solemnity and self-mastery. We are boldness. We are order. We are depth. How could we belong here? No way. But let's continue celebrating ourselves now just for the joy of it, even though the point is made. Celebrating ourselves is ecstasy: it's how we became human.

We are language, science and philosophy, the use of wind and fire, the body of traditional knowledge, the elaboration of procreation into courtship and romance. Because of us the planet is enriched with the hearth and the home, the farmhouse, the lighthouse, the monastery and the observatory, the garden and the park, the harbor, the temple and the theatre, the school, the library, the hospital and the museum, the village and the village square, the tribe, the clan, the town and the city. We invented agriculture, navigation, choreography and the healing arts: architecture, costume and cuisine. All these, our idea.

We are the sailor and the midwife, the wood-carver and the sage, the tinker, the builder and the troubadour, the fisherman and the weaver, the stonemason and the priest, the craftsman, the peasant, the bandit and the nurse, the lover, the teacher, the neighbor and the friend, and a thousand more. Out of our inconceivable effort, and at our inconceivable cost, emerged the human personality: that being which can hold together in consciousness a meaningful world: that being whose ability to love makes it divine.

Ecstacy. Now let's hit our stride.

We can know the truth. We can do the good. We have a sense of beauty and a sense of justice. We know that human life is a moral drama, and we know why. Only in our souls is revealed the holiness of what is: Creation, and the holiness of what ought to be: the Law. The theological virtues are sacrifice, detachment and humility, faith, hope and charity: we discovered them: we realized what they were: we made them our devotion. We are committed to ourselves without reservation: our name is tenacity. If nothing were known of us except that we bury our dead and kneel at the grave, that fact alone would tell it all.

Escape? There's no escape. It just isn't our style.

Was Fidel Really Crazy When He Was In The Mountains?

When the definitions of victory and defeat are obvious, energy is joyous. We move without hesitation. We become vivid and unpredictable, even to ourselves. This state awaits us in every moment: all we need is clear vision.

What is clear vision?

Solidarity.

Facing a Few of the Facts

Introduction

Facing a Few of the Facts was the thirteenth paper on the program. I believe Louis di Prima was invited to participate in the Conference for the same reason I was engaged to edit the papers: we are a bridge to the mainland of educated non-specialist readers to whom this book is addressed. I include his paper, however, on its own merits entirely.

Louis di Prima was born in 1938 and has his B.A. in English Literature from New York University. He has written several books of poetry and an extended prose-poem on the life on cetaceans; his plays have been performed in New York City and San Francisco by the City's Edge Theatre.

Mr. di Prima, in my opinion, speaks for a part of all of us, although a part we rarely reveal and perhaps rarely admit even to ourselves. It is the darker side, the realistic pessimism, the ironic despair, the gallows humor in most thoughtful people which Mr. di Prima has chosen to express in his paper. He has articulated attitudes and feelings common to nearly everyone in the nuclear age. I hope the reader will understand that I have no intention of patronizing his or her sensibilities, through drawing attention to the obvious, when I pay homage to the writer's skill by observing that beneath the ironic gaiety of Mr. di Prima's despair is a concern, indeed a grief, and a commitment to truth, as profound as any expressed in this book.

Mr. di Prima, dressed casually as usual, delivered his paper with calm restraint, conscious, it appeared to me, of the anomaly of his presence at the Conference and of the slight shock caused among some of the participants by an intrusion of the vernacular style. An engrossed silence fell upon the hall, however, after he was about five minutes into his

presentation, and when he finished there was, I think to
everyone's surprise, a round of applause amounting nearly
to an ovation. I believe we were applauding an almost appall-
ing honesty.

That night I made the following entry in my journal. By
this time I was becoming aware that my experience at the
Conference was going to extend beyond my professional
responsibilities.

> There's a certain excitement building up here, not alto-
> gether unpleasant and destined, I suspect, to be increasingly
> insistent, and I must confess to being uncertain whether it's in
> the atmosphere or in my own mind. Perhaps a bit of both.
>
> Due to the industry, I am tempted to say ferocity, of the
> scholars assembled here one almost feels the entire world to be
> present. One senses the pressure of an immense silent audience
> as well as the distant roar of an immense vague seething
> activity, the work of the world, throbbing away "out there" on
> the crisis-ridden globe whose image is being remorselessly
> painted, in all its significant forms and hues, by scholarship
> and bibliographies—and by a truly astonishing creativity as
> well. The global crisis, which is also a "crisis" for each of us as
> individuals, no matter how assiduously we may strive for
> Eastern detachment, is being brought to life here. Mr. di
> Prima, by focussing our attention so fixedly upon "the end of
> the world," has apparently succeeded—where the previous
> papers have met with a certain effective resistance—in estab-
> lishing the sense of a collective destiny and, I think, a collective
> alarm, which is simultaneously personal as well. (Another
> instance of "the two which are really one?") We are definitely
> not in an ivory tower here at Sandstone.
>
> And yet of course we are. Our experience here is made up
> entirely of words. The world is being evoked by the magic of
> language, and it is the purity of this verbal evocation, its
> elimination of all extraneous details and day-to-day distrac-
> tions, which is so striking: this purity, indeed, is the salient

aspect of the Conference. It is precisely this kind of purification
of reality, accessible in all forms of solitary retreat, which best
provides one, if he chooses to avail himself of it, with the
opportunity to appraise his own life and situation. And what
we discover, perhaps against our will, is not that we may
become involved in larger realities than our private lives—
social, political, even "spiritual"—but that we are somehow
already "involved," already implicated. Is this not, when all
is said and done, the fundamental assumption of all the papers
we have heard? Of Dr. Harrison's blunt observation that "in
our essence we are the universe"? Of Dr. Frank's entire
cosmology?

It is, of course, inevitable that in the presence of so many
cultivated intelligences, and such intense intellectual engage-
ments, one would feel propelled toward introspection and,
paradoxically enough, toward a more vivid recognition of the
outer world as well, with its ambiguous, almost tantalizing,
messages, proposals and supplications. Is there, at the very
center of every consciousness here, a growing sense of desperation? Of imminent destruction? Is detachment possible, or
ethical, or desirable? Or wise? These questions come to mind. I
find myself speculating, not without certain misgivings, that
my inner life may perhaps become more "intense" in the
future—without, of course, any sacrifice of that external
continuity and regularity whose benefits, and necessity,
become progressively obvious as we mature.

. . . Something is evading me. I believe I am becoming
aware, or trying not to become aware, that an irreversible
change has taken place in me here at Sandstone. Yes; I think
that's what has happened. It is disquieting—even, I must
confess, saddening—for one who has lived a more or less
private life, as I have, especially since Helen passed away, to
realize that he has experienced an unforeseen alteration of
intellectual perspective from which there is no turning back.
One fears a temporary faltering of equilibrium or loss of
self-possession. That the alteration is undoubtedly in the

nature of an emergence, or expansion, or even awakening, does little to diminish the sense of apprehension.

But I am in the midst of it now. It occupies the whole of my concentration, and therefore it is magnified. This has happened before. My life, gratefully, is erected upon a sturdy foundation, and can doubtless easily absorb, and even welcome, a bit of personal growth. I am reacting more to the unexpectedness of it than to its actual import, which can only be positive.

And what is that import, exactly? Simple prudence demands that we be precise in such matters. I think I have discovered that my life, my "true self," as it were, is rather larger than I thought it was, that it extends beyond, indeed far beyond, the boundaries I have both carefully and arbitrarily marked out, the fences I have so industriously erected, and always so hastily repaired. (I recall Dr. Rosenblatt's remark that the self does not end at the skin.) Its true dimensions, as a matter of fact, are almost dizzying to contemplate.

Facing a Few of the Facts

by Louis di Prima

Something Big is going to happen! Something Big is going to happen! We have to prepare!

What is it? What's going to happen?

I don't know!

Then how can we prepare? How can we prepare for it if we don't know what it is?

I don't know! I don't know! Just prepare, that's all! Prepare!

*

The guru tells you about the Great Truth that remains the same throughout all eternity while everything else just comes and goes.

The prophet tells you you're in big trouble and it's going to get much worse if you don't clean up your act, and maybe it's too late anyway.

The commissar tells you what you're going to do for your own good whether you want to or not.

The revolutionary tells you your hour has come and nothing can stop you now.

The shrinks and their cousins tell you whatever you pay them to tell you.

The leaders, the newspapers and the TV tell you lies, lies, lies.

Where will you turn, baby, *where will you turn?*

*

The headlines are not reassuring. You laugh at them, shaking your head with gentle disbelief, and then forget them. Who really gives a shit anymore? Who can be seriously concerned about a situation so utterly hopeless?

Only the well-intentioned fools, filled with outrage or alarm, who never seem to realize that all they're really doing with their efforts to save the world is throwing their own little twig into the conflagration, adding their little squeak to the roar.

Fools. Are they really fools? Or are they the salt of the earth, the models, the heroes and heroines who point the way for the rest of us?

Who can say what they are? Or what anyone is. The bottom's dropped out of the world.

*

What are you going to do? I mean *really:* what are you going to do? Do you actually believe anything is going to stop the drift toward disaster? The drift of an entire planet? Do you actually believe we're going to be saved? Everything is heading straight to hell, the whole thing is falling apart, the whole world is going insane. Do you really believe all this can be halted or reversed? *It's too late, It's all over. Just dig it.* Everything was always headed this way, building up to this—we can see that now—and we're the ones privileged to watch it happen. We're the generation privileged to know the whole story, the whole drama, from the beginning to the end. We're going to see the curtain come down. Our understanding of humanity is the most profound. What difference does it make if it ends now or in a million years?

*

The whole past, every bit of it, everything that ever happened, is entirely vanished, gone completely. Whatever fragments survive exist only in our memories, and then only when we're actually remembering them, only in the living moment in which they are actually being remembered. The future, of course, also doesn't exist. No past, no future.

Nothing exists but this living moment, right now, and even this moment, like memories of the past or anticipations of the future, is only held there by our minds.

So what is lost, and who loses anything, if the world comes to an end?

*

Many decent responsible people seem to have decided to face the end enjoying music and screwing. If there's nothing we can do about it, what's wrong with celebrating life right up to the end, along with the rest of nature? Other decent responsible people shuffle around with downcast eyes and troubled expressions; they hope they'll be able to confront certain death with the dignity appropriate to a noble being in its hour of tragedy. Like the captain and the crew singing hymns on the deck of a sinking ship. Still others, also decent, also responsible, are determined to go down fighting, defiant to the last.

It'll be business as usual, however. Business as usual. Our ordinary nervous daily lives, nothing quite settled and nothing quite appropriate, exploded into sheer screaming terror. Don't you think so? Sure. And it's OK. Who are you to be critical?

*

Now you could say that we have to save the world for the sake of future generations, so humanity can continue to evolve toward its divine destiny, or that we have to save the world to keep the faith with past generations, so that their labor will not have been in vain. In either case, it's humanity itself we're supposed to be concerned about, "Humanity" with a capital H. Something bigger than you and me, in other words.

But you could also say fuck that way of thinking. Unless

we choose to make them an issue, the dead and the unborn
are out of the picture completely. They have nothing to lose,
they don't suffer, and we don't owe them anything. There's
nobody but us; we are what's at stake. We're the ones, we
and our children, who have to figure out how to face this
incredible nightmare. All by ourselves, and *for* ourselves.

*

Just think of it: the dead are going to kill the living! We're
not doing this to ourselves. It's the momentum of the history
they made, and the damage they did, that's going to kill us.
We're not committing suicide, we're being murdered. By the
dead! Talk about bad karma!

In the whole history of humanity, there have only been
two human situations. The one that ended about fifty years
ago, and ours.

True, there were other times when people thought the
world was going to come to an end, although of course they
were wrong. But it was always for a good reason, always as
part of the scheme of things. Divine retribution, the end of a
cosmic cycle, the arrival of the Kingdom of Heaven—there
was always a meaning, so it was always acceptable.

But our situation is different.

Or at least it appears to be.

*

It's really just a question of style; there's no right and
wrong in a terminal situation. Different people will face the
end in different ways, that's all. There's nothing unworthy
or debased in refusing to think about a calamity so immense,
so beyond our comprehension; it's not more "elevated" to
look it in the face than to ignore it. We're not morally
required to try to save the world. To eat, drink and be merry
is not shameful any more that to join organizations is ex-

emplary. Everyone has a right to their way, and every way is just as human as every other way: they're all human—fully, completely, totally human. Make your choice, play your role, respect everyone.

*

Existence is clearly a gift. We have done nothing to earn or deserve it, so we have no right to complain if it is withdrawn. For awhile, we existed. For awhile, there was something rather than nothing, and that something was clearly a miracle glorious beyond glory, and we, whatever "we" are, woven somehow into that miracle, are a "place" where it becomes aware of itself. More could be said about all this, but it would just be glory heaped upon glory. The proper response in the recipient of a gift is gratitude.

*

You keep thinking that maybe somehow everybody's going to pull it together at the last minute and save the world. A rally in the eleventh hour. The whole human race suddenly realizes it's now or never, and in one stupendous spiritual and physical exertion actually rises to meet the occasion. But at the same time you know this is a fantasy. You know what people are like, and you know what we're up against.

We became five billion interchangeable parts in one giant death machine and anything we do on the scale of the death machine's power is just more machinery. That's cold reality, feet on the ground. The ways we came to think and live and work, the end we created for ourselves by thinking and living and working in those ways, and the various ways in which we then confront that end *all add up to one life style:* it's all one reality, in other words, one circular dynamic. Preparing our end and confronting our end are the same process. To oppose our actual way of facing it with some fantasy about how we might save ourselves is nonsense: the situation and the response are a single reality, they cannot be separated. It could even be argued that this is the only way it could have happened, that all along, from the very beginning, this was our only destiny. Who knows? But look around you: you don't see what *should* be and you don't see what *shouldn't* be: you see what *followed*.

*

"What will we tell the children?"
A silly question. The children already know. Knowledge of the end is in the air we breathe, in every moment of our lives, every glance and tone of voice, every institution, artifact and encounter. We grow into it as naturally and inevitably as we grow into physical maturity. Knowledge of the end is everything, this whole reality. You don't have to worry about "telling the children." You can stop whining. We've already told them. With matchless eloquence.

*

You look at the pavement and imagine weeds, the same weeds we see now, sprouting through acres of rubble and up-ended slabs, gradually covering the lower levels of evidence. Except at the "epicenter"—one of our new words— the skeletons of buildings will still stand, maybe tipped a bit from the vertical. And of course there'll be automobile wreckage everywhere—chassis, engines, bumpers, seat springs: probably strips of fused rubber baked into the cement. And bones. There'll be bones. Bombed-out cities. Silent streets.
The urban environment is beginning to appear temporary. We know that soon the Earth will be moving in again, so beautiful and calm. It'll cover up all this shit. New things will be born.

You look up at the sky. It's going to split open and explode from horizon to horizon. We all glance speculatively up at the sky now, from time to time: not in actual fear, but because *that's where it will come from.*

*

You love so many things about life, there's so much to love. Is that why the end seems so terrible? Because all those things will be no more? Singing, laughing, swimming, loving, the sight and taste of Earth's numberless marvels, the never-ending shower of miracles: *everything:* the whole soaring mind-blowing ecstasy of just *being* here, in a *universe, digging it.* All those wonderful beautiful things, gone forever. Or is it the suffering? The moaning mutilated survivors, begging for water, the terrible radiation sicknesses, the agony of children? Or is it simply the personal fear of pain and death? Or is it just the great colossal tragedy of it, the waste, the senseless destruction?

Or are you one of those pugnacious types, completely disillusioned with human beings, who really doesn't care? Too full of a kind of sullen battle-hardened self-respect to waste your time talking a lot of crap about all these things no one is going to do anything about anyway. You're part of the picture also. Tough as nails. You've been around. You look people straight in the eye, you know the bastards are lying and you don't back off an inch. Belligerent: you stick your chin out. And just like any of the rest of us you might die while you're "on hold," listening to Muzak or a recording, impatiently tapping on an ashtray with your ball-point pen. Lots of people will die "on hold," fuming with vexation, enraged that they might have been forgotten, trying to keep from slamming the phone down and losing their place in line and having to start all over again. What a way to die!

*

If this is the end, we ought to exit in style: we ought to flaunt an undaunted spirit before the eyes of the universe. We should leave in processions, dressed in costumes, strutting and shaking tambourines, drinking beer and tossing roses, with flags and floats, brass bands, jazz bands and cheer leaders setting the rhythm, like a Mardi Gras parade. All the cultures of the world represented, all our magnificent achievements. A festival of humanity. The gods are skeptical about us, you know; they scratch their chins and exchange glances. We ought to leave them something to remember us by. We screwed up, no doubt about it. But when we were great we were the greatest: no one could hold a candle to us. We've got class, pride, guts and soul. We've got *verve.* We're not going to look like losers. Right? Let's show them how the *humans* bow out. In style!

*

You don't want to fight on either side. A plague on both their houses! You just want to be left alone. When history comes rapping on the door you want to sneak out the window and slip away into the hills till it's all over. Live on the Earth where nothing ever happens: no history, no progress, no nothing: just the four seasons, the sun, the soil and the sky.

You don't need the slogans and the programs. You don't need the parties, movements, alliances, coalitions and committees, the meetings, conferences and conventions, the leaflets and pamphlets, the angry or jubilant fanatics screaming from the podium. There's a vicious unconscious menace lurking behind all political passion: you can see it in the way they size you up. Violence, verbal or real: that's all it is. Power: the struggle for power and the continuous identification of enemies. No matter how solemnly they may abjure it, no matter how loudly they may deplore it, political people have secretly reconciled themselves to carnage: that was the real decision they made: all the rest is excuses.

So avoid history. Stay out of it, keep a low profile, duck and hide. Be committed to life. History is just one long tormented agonized march to hell. Can't they see it? Can't they see they're all part of the same death trip, no matter which side they're on? History is madness, suffering and madness: we're either conscripted into it or our allegiance is seduced and then betrayed. Stay out of it. Have the guts to say no to a noble cause. Be a history dodger. Everybody else is going to die.

You just want to be left alone, that's all. But you know there's no escape. There are no hills to hide in. There are no hills any more. It's just a matter of time. You pound the table now and then in wild-eyed defiance, but inwardly you crumpled long ago. You shuffle through one week after another. At twilight, seated by the window, you raise a haggard glare toward the fading light and pray.

*

Right up to the very end people will still be going through the motions. That's what's so incredible about it. Everything we do is unreal, everything is bullshit, madness and hell, yet nothing can break the spell that keeps it going. We're all like mechanical dolls, busily puttering and scurrying around, completely absorbed in our own little worlds—and if we ever glance over our shoulders, hastily, vaguely startled, at the giant shadow of death looming bigger and darker on the horizon every day, we only return to those little private worlds, those dreamy feverish pursuits, with a resolution even more urgent, an energetic absorption even more desperate, as if the only response to a horrible reality is an even more single-minded devotion to fantasy. You could also say that people become so totally overwhelmed by the pressure of survival, as the pace speeds up and conditions deteriorate, that they simply lose the ability to stand back and get an overview, they can't break the grip of the details, they can't stop running—not that it would make any difference anyway. At any rate, there's no way to stop the pretense because there's no way to stop the machine.

And all this, it should be quite clear, is no one's fault. There's no guilt and no responsibility. Everyone's doing their level best. This is the way things happen at the end, that's all. If people could do something about it, if we could act, it wouldn't be the end!

*

Every now and then you think of someone you know as a person who is also, just like you, living at the time of the end, and you realize, as you must and with humble irony, that sharing this fate is now your deepest bond with other people, the new and final foundation of our common humanity. Take anyone you know, look at them from this point of view, and you see them as they really are.

Take a very simple example. Someone's seated in a restaurant absorbed in the menu, trying to decide what he wants to eat for dinner that night. So many things look delicious! How to choose? He laughs helplessly and a bit self-consciously at his dilemma, aware of the disparity between the intentness of his approach and the triviality of the occasion, and, offering absurd suggestions and beginning to feel impatient, everyone jokes about his gluttony, his indecisiveness of character, his well-known history of vacillation and ambivalence. Finally he throws up his hands and plunges into a selection, the waiter wearily smiles, rolling his eyes, and the subject of discussion changes instantly. Everyone is animated.

Innocence. While all this was going on you suddenly thought of the end and the word that came to mind was innocence. He finally decided on spaghetti and meatballs, his original enthusiasm before all the other dishes caught his eye, and he looked sad and preoccupied when everyone filed out.

Innocent. Therefore condemned. We eat, we drink, we screw, we sleep. We're simple. We can only handle a small scene. A handful of people is all we'll ever remember, a handful of people is all we'll have time enough to love. A circle of friends, a family. One face, just one face, can overwhelm us! History, the immensity of history . . . it's beyond us. It baffles us. Confused, suspicious, vaguely insulted, we refuse to budge, we just hold our own: with dignity. Everyone likes to eat out now and then.

But the thought goes further. In this smallness our strength resides. It's our native ground. Our stronghold—for whatever that's worth.

*

You go on trying to do things the right way even though there doesn't seem to be any point in it anymore. Maybe it's the instinct of good workmanship. Or maybe it's because you know how terrible the alternative is: character rot: your personality disintegrates and you become some kind of bum or degenerate. One of those people who smile confidently but plead with their eyes at the same time; you can't tell whether they're begging for help or hoping you won't see through the facade: it's probably both. A tremendous variety of human types flower at the end, all sorts of people, all sorts of improbable combinations. The end is a great stimulus to individuality.

But you have to go on trying, you have to keep the faith. Even when everything seems futile. The end is a great challenge. We have to struggle to speak, to explain things, articulate ideas, when the whole world to which the words refer is about to be destroyed; we have to exhaust ourselves in endless haggling about right and wrong, in endless disputes which always become insane as the night wears on because the world in which the dispute takes place is itself insane; we have to throw ourselves into all sorts of endeavors haunted by the bitter sinking certainty that there'll be something flawed or false in them every step of the way, something empty no matter how sincere our effort, because the substance has dropped out of life, because nothing is ever what it seems to be anymore. The end is a *great* challenge! It brings out the best in us!

*

Listening to music now is no small thing. If there are any survivors interested in reminiscing about how it happened, they'll certainly spend some time talking about the role of music at the end.

Think of it this way:

We can hear the same piece of music as many times as we want to, and each time it's the same: each time is the *same* time. Each time we hear it we escape from linear one-way time and enter into the eternal present of cosmic time, an eternal continually repeatable *now*: we enter another world, a world outside of time, the timeless world of the music. Music, in other words, *defies the end*. Listening to music we escape from history, which is precisely what we long to do every minute of our lives.

No wonder we turn to music almost religiously! It's a refuge and a consolation, beautiful, invulnerable and untranslatable, within and without at once, at once nowhere and everywhere, as faithful to us as we are to it. Music is instantly aware of every secret huddling fretful and desolate in our souls; it speaks to our every mood and weather, even those of which we aren't conscious; it offers itself fully and indiscriminately to everyone who approaches it with a pure heart, regardless of their past deeds. It calms our troubled devotion, uplifts our battered spirits, pacifies our bewildered weariness and renews our will to live. It allows us to forget. We love it, we love those who write and perform it for us, we can't imagine life without it. We stumble home from work, exhausted and tense, and head straight for the stereo. First things first.

And what does all this remind us of? You guessed it! Music is just like God! They must have something to do with Each Other!

*

You try to be aware of the subtle changes, the insidious gradual transformations that go on unnoticed till all of a sudden one day you pause, look around yourself stunned, and realize you've been living in a dream—as if some huge vicious animal had been creeping up soundlessly behind you all along, inch by inch, waiting till it was close enough to pounce. You try, but life is very tricky; it's hard to stay on top of things.

There's nothing inside holding it all together. That's the problem. Anything can happen. Anybody can do anything. No matter how crazy or far out it is, there's always an argument to defend it. Always an excuse, a point of view, a new interpretation.

You try to stay on top of things, you try to protect your life. But there are snipers smirking in every tree, training their sights on you. Ambushes and imposters. Treachery. Who knows what your kids will drop on your lap tomorrow? Who knows what's happening right this minute that'll make you mutter a year from now, ruefully, "I wish I'd seen it coming"? You hunger for something sacred. Some changeless truth avowed by everyone, something clean and pure and shining and untouchable, everlasting, that isn't even in the same world as all this shit. Another world completely. Something absolutely the opposite of this.

There's nothing you can rely on here. That's the trouble. There's no foundation, nothing you can rely on.

*

Graduation ceremonies always make you think of the end.
The irony of the word "commencement"! It's too much. The
feeling is most poignant, of course, if it's an elementary
school. All the bright shining faces, the girls flouncing
around in their party dresses and the boys trying to sit still
on the stage, everyone chattering, darting, breathless with
secrets. No problem more urgent than stifling laughter.
What obscene madness can have possessed us? What devil
from hell? You fight back tears. All these little people, so
bursting with life.

Life, life, life. A whole planet teeming with life. How did it
ever happen? What's it all for? From the individual point of
view the aim is a completed life span: just live out the allotted
span of life. But there's a larger picture, we are told, a larger
truth. What can that be? There's just no way to know.

*

When you think about it now, with the so-called struggles
of the sixties a full decade behind you, when you really try to
envision what might save us or emerge victorious from the
wreckage, one thing, at least, is clear: it won't be anything
organized and goal oriented. Forget that. It won't be an
organization or a party or a movement or any of that kind of
crap. It won't have a plan or a purpose or a program and it
won't think about means and ends. It won't think at all, as a
matter of fact. It won't be future oriented. All that stuff is
where we die: it's history. You can see that now. No regrets,
but you can see that.

You've decided, instead, that the world will be saved by
people who aren't trying to save it. You've watched them in
action. Now you smile when you're alone, confident, detached, serene—although you never really feel alone anymore. You don't hope, you don't fear, you no longer worry
about survival. You've seen something. There's no way to
describe it. Either you see it or you don't. It's everywhere, it's

everything, it's invisible to the eye, and the thing that acts most like it is grass. Just plain old grass.

*

So what if we become mutants after a holocaust? What's a mutant, anyway? Maybe we're mutants right now. Whatever adapts belongs there, that's the way it works. If it's alive and kicking, Good Luck to it. Good Luck, you funny-looking thing! Hang in there! Life is beautiful!

*

How do the politicians become insane? How do they become the enemies of the human race? It's really incredible when you think about it. Why doesn't just *one* of them ever go sane in public, crack up under the pressure or actually plan it in advance, and start screaming the truth at a press conference, just *one* of them? Why hasn't it happened? Are they really androids, plastic robots? Have they been drugged? By whom? Are they pre-selected and trained by some secret organization? How do they learn to smile and talk that way? It's truly a miracle: a testimony to our limitless potentials. And that's just the politicians. If you try to imagine where the "military leaders" come from you could *really* go out of you mind! Those guys are *not like us*!

*

People come up with some pretty far-fetched ideas at the end. We are urged, for example, in response to the emptiness that invades our souls, to share our real feelings and express our emotions freely. Then we won't feel lonely. We're also urged to have fun—just do anything that makes you feel good, it doesn't make any difference what it is. Be happy. Some people, on the other hand, prescribe hard work to reclaim our errant spirits from self-indulgence. Everyone has an answer. There's no shortage of answers.

You smile: faintly, contemptuously, wearily, remotely. Answers. Emptiness. Childishness. You'll just live your life out, that's all. There are things that must be done regardless of circumstances. These are the things you'll do.

*

Everything that happens now is a portent. Economic trends, protests, "scientific breakthroughs," murders, election returns, nuclear and chemical developments, teenage styles, musical styles, the latest statistics, the latest bizarre stories, the academy awards, official announcements . . . everything points toward some kind of breakdown. Toward chaos. Every new piece of information jibes with all the others, every detail confirms the thesis, every event is new evidence. We nod with grim satisfaction. The universal premonition is validated without fail.

Strange to live in such times. Actually eerie. You wonder what it was like to live before all this happened, before it fell apart, when the world made sense and there was a scheme of things and everything had its proper place. Tragedies could befall us, and certainly did, there was evil, but nothing could threaten the foundation: that was impregnable. No matter what happened, people must have felt basically secure: the ground beneath their feet remained firm. They had confidence. That was probably the fundamental feeling. Confidence. Faith. Confidence in what, though? You can't even imagine what they had confidence in! Order? Justice? God? Probably God.

*

If there's a nuclear holocaust, what will be remembered? Who will be doing the remembering? In what kind of setting? Filthy men and women wrapped in scorched blankets, huddled over fires kindled from the debris of incomprehensible ruins, whispering, in desperate awe, the fearful explanations of their wild-eyed sages? Mutants, only approximately human, lisping the conjectures of approximately human brains? Who knows? Maybe the damage will be much more restricted. But if the self-consciousness of world civilization is annihilated with its technology, or drastically degraded, which seems likely, humanity, or its descendants, will probably only remember that there was once a terrible fiery calamity of some kind, a great Judgment or Day of Reckoning given as punishment for some cosmic transgression. It'll become a myth. A myth about pride, a lesson in humility. Which is what it really is, of course. A lesson in humility. On the other hand, it might be remembered as the consequence of a sneak attack, long foreseen and feared, launched by the Russians—or the Americans or the Chinese, the communists or the bourgeoisie. That would be too bad. Wouldn't it?

*

Maybe the cities *ought* to be destroyed. Did you ever think of that? Maybe they no longer advance the cause of life, if they ever did, and it's time for them to be recalled. Removed, like tumors, from the face of the Earth they disfigure. Maybe some great surgeon in the sky, a close friend of Mother Nature, is pulling on his rubber gloves right now and selecting the scalpel. It's been argued that these things take care of themselves, you know: that the world strives for balance and harmony and that in the long run equilibrium is always restored. "Whatever goes against the Tao will not last long."

Crazy talk. But with the ring of truth. Think of it: the cities are where history is made. And it's history that's coming to an end. History, cities, death. Death of all kinds. What do you go to the country for? What are you trying to get away from?

*

Sometimes you speculate that key people may rebel at the last minute, just flat out disobey orders, refuse to push the buttons that fire the missiles. You wonder about it. A spontaneous mutiny in the name of sanity: they just won't be able to go through with it. Maybe; but don't count on it. These people have been very carefully trained. "Programmed" would be more precise: they're not really "people" as we ordinarily use the word. Anyway, you can be quite sure that this contingency has been foreseen and the appropriate safeguards incorporated into the system. They're thorough, our friends in the "command centers." They know about "the human factor." They've studied it from every angle, with great sympathy. Even with compassion. Genuine compassion.

*

What you imagine when you think of the end is the wild flight from the cities. Millions of people scrambling to their cars in a frenzy of terror, hurling children and food into the back seats and leaping behind the wheel, millions of cars smashing into each other at intersections in the mad race for the freeways, fist fights at every telephone, knives and bullets at every gas station, the air filled with smoke, sirens, gunshots and screams. The missiles are on their way.

This picture is printed on everyone's mind. It doesn't take very much imagination. And as for the aftermath, maybe you saw the films taken by Japanese cameramen in Hiroshima and Nagasaki. No words can describe it. No philosophy, no spiritual posture, no human resource whatever, is equal to it. Whan the lights go on everyone is silent, in tears.

You inhabit this reality. If you could think your way around it or above it or through it or out of it, you would— but you can't. The mind stops right here, at the end. It makes perfect sense not to think about it.

*

You see it this way, you see it that way, you see it any way you want to see it, you don't see it at all. It's the end of the world.

I'm a good person, I'm a humanitarian person, I love the planet, I love people, I want everybody to be happy. I want peace. But this thing has gotten out of hand. . . . There's just no way to fit it into my schedule. . . . Sure, sometimes I lie awake at night wondering what's going to happen to the good old human race. I worry about it. So what? I fall asleep, I wake up in the morning, I go back to work. What else am I supposed to do? . . . I love it all. I love the whole thing, the whole planet and everything on it, especially the oceans, I love water, but I love it all really and if this is the end, well, it's just the end. Right? Everything comes to an end. . . . I just can't get into it. I mean I just can't get all that worked up about it. . . . I think about the children. Why should they have to die? They're innocent. No future for them. It's not fair. I don't care so much about myself, I've lived a little, I've seen life, you know? But the kids should have a chance. I have kids. . . . Yeah, I know the world's coming to an end. Who doesn't? I just don't have time to worry about that right now. I have my own problems to deal with. . . . It's like Rome. It's the fall of the Roman Empire all over again. History repeats itself. You never step into the same river twice. It's a cycle. Over and over again. The same things. Here today, gone tomorrow. . . . Well, I think our President's doing the best he can. We have to be strong to defend ourselves, and they have to know it. That's the only way to preserve peace. I know it's a terrible way, but it's all we can do right now. . . . Sometimes I just wish the bombs would fall already, just get it all over with. . . . I'm just going to live my life out, that's all. I'm going to hope for the best. It's bigger than I am. . . . I just can't bear to think about it. It's too terrible, just too terrible. I cry when I think about it. I just cry. I lie in bed at night and cry. Sometimes even during the day, when I'm alone. . . . Well, I don't know. I don't know that there's any point in getting so excited about it. Letting it interfere with your life. I mean, why? What are you going to do about it? . . . It's a judgment, that's all. It's a judgment. You break the rules, you pay for it. You sow and you reap. It's a law. . . . I never talk about it because it's too emotional, you know? But sometimes I think maybe we should all talk about it. Maybe we could do something then. I don't know. . . . I feel terrible. But what can I do? What can I do? Little me! . . . Sometimes I think, why did I have to live in this time? Why was I born in this time? I'm not meant to be here. . . . Sure, but what's it got to do with me? What's it got to do with me? What do you want from me? I'm nobody. Mister Nobody . . . If it ever happens, you know, the missiles, the warheads, whatever they are, the holocaust and all that, I'm sure I'll be totally terrified, just freak out completely. I'll probably die of fear. But in a way it all seems so unreal. It just seems unreal. It's hard to take it seriously. . . . I've heard about it, I know about it, now just leave me alone. What do you expect me to say? . . . I don't think I can die. I know it sounds crazy, but I just know I won't die completely. Some part of me will go on living. Nothing ever dies. My friends say I'm a mystic. . . . It makes me love everything even more. Isn't that the way it should be? I mean I just love everything now, I love life, I love people. I love New Orleans. If it's going to be the end of the world we should love it while we have the chance. . . . I know everybody thinks about it. I just know, even though we never talk about it. It's our shared secret. I can tell. I have insight. . . . I think we should go in there first. First strike. We can do it. They're just holding back because of the communists in government. Nobody wants to admit it, but it's true. They can't hide it anymore. People are beginning to open their eyes. . . . Once I asked my father if he ever thought about it. He looked away and mumbled something.

I couldn't catch it. I think he said sometimes. I never asked him again. My mother told me not to talk about it. . . . We don't need those pesticides. We don't need all those chemicals. Cancer, hydrogen bombs. Pollution. It's sick. The whole world is sick. I don't know how it happened. It's money, really. Money's behind it all. The almighty dollar. . . . I just hope it happens after I'm gone. I know that sounds terribly selfish, but I really feel that way. I don't want to see it. I want to die with hope. . . . Oh I don't know. When you gotta go, you gotta go. Right? I live with it. I doesn't stop me from enjoying life. I enjoy life right up to the hilt. And then some! . . . It was science. Too much science. Not enough humanity. . . . I think about my future. I plan for it. I don't just give up and not work for anything because the world may come to and end. Nothing is without risk. I don't throw in the towel. The world is beyond my control. I'm not. That's my philosophy. . . . Oh we deserve it. People are so stupid. If they're going to do all these terrible things, they deserve what they get. . . . Well what do you expect me to do about it? Walk right into Russia and tell them to throw all those bombs away? They'd shoot me on the spot! . . . . You just look at it. Overpopulation, the military situation, all this violence, the hot spots, the economy, the build-up. Nuclear power. The hawks. Where else can it go? Right? Star wars. You can see it coming. It's inevitable. . . . I used to dream about a good life. A good clean life, decent, you know what I mean? Neighbors, friends, everybody helping everybody else, a good environment for the kids. Forget it. . . . It's greed. Everybody wants it all for themselves. Instead of sharing, working things out, they try to get it all. Me first, number one. So there's tension. Everybody's afraid. A cold war. Bigger bombs. Then one day, Bang! It's all over. Just like the cave men. . . . Think of all this suicide. There's much more of that then you think. Why? Because they have no hope. They see no future. They see no reason to go on living. . . . The pollution is slow, the nuclear war is fast.

That's the only difference. It's all going the same way. . . . It
makes me appreciate everything more. I see how precious
everything is. Every moment. I wouldn't have realized. I
don't take anything for granted now. I'm more open. . . . I'm
ready for it. If it's going to happen I'm going to be ready for
it. That's the way I live my life. Take it as it comes. . . . It's
just disgusting. It's tragic. Sometimes I think it's all a bad
dream. I just refuse to admit it into my life. . . . Well, it's one
of those things that everybody knows about but we just
can't do anything about it. . . . Once I really looked it in the
face. I can't explain it. But I know there isn't any end. It just
isn't the end. It's something else. It's just the way things are,
that's all. . . . It won't be so bad. A lot of this is exaggerated.
Everybody won't die. We'll rebuild. Like they did overseas
after World War Two. Now you go over there, you wouldn't
even know there was a war. . . . This was all predicted. It's in
the Bible. All you have to do is read the Bible. . . . I hate
them. I hate the people who are doing this to us and to our
children. To the environment. I don't see why they're
allowed to live. They have no right to live. . . . I used to care
but now I don't. What's the use? . . . How do you know who
to believe? Everybody tells you something different. Everybody's got their line. Interest groups, special interests. The
war machine, the ecology people. The oil companies. Even
the doctors lie. . . . If it happens it's God's Will. We don't
have to understand it. It's beyond us. . . . I still have hope.
I'm one of the crazy idealists who still have hope. We'll pull
out of it. We always have. We still have free will. . . . We've
abused the Earth. We've abused Creation. Our societies
have been irresponsible. We've lived by false values. Now it's
all coming back at us. . . . It's a pretty messed-up world. I
think about it a lot. I don't have any easy answers. . . . Yeah,
it's my life! My one and only life! I want to live! . . . Once
someone whispered to me in a bus that the world was
coming to an end. I was embarrassed. I didn't know what to
say. But I never forgot her. I remember her face.

Homage To Reality:
How It Looks To Those Who Can See It

Introduction

Sister Angela Maria Prescott, the senior participant at the Conference, was born in 1899 in Viareggio, Italy. She received her Ph.D in Theology from Fordham University in 1930 and a doctorate in Eastern Religions from Notre Dame in 1951. After World War II she served on the faculty of the University of Rome for two years, and in 1955 she received the Christopher Award for Catholic Scholarship, from the University of Dublin, for a monumental comparative study of Spanish and Sufi mysticism. At the time she delivered her paper, as it turned out, she had only three months left to live. She died in October at the Convent of the Sacred Heart, in the foothills of the Blue Ridge Mountains, where she had spent most of her life.

Sister Angela's paper, the fifteenth on the program, was among the briefest presented to the Conference. Originating in a mind sufficiently disengaged from "this world," it fairly defies categorization and challenges the resources of commentary. Resorting to terms whose simplicity, compared with the polyphonic rhythms and harmonies of Sister Angela's exquisite English prose, seems almost vulgar, we may summarize her paper as an invocation of the indestructible spiritual reality, composed of the "permanent archetypes," which lies beneath and manifests itself as the transient material world. This changeless reality, surviving the inevitable degeneration and death of all material things at the end of a "cosmic cycle," becomes visible to the seers and saints and in their vision presages the rebirth which always follows. This time of death and rebirth, according to Sister

Angela's breathtaking perspective, defines our present situation: it is, in other words, nothing less than what we in our provincial terminology and limited understanding have been calling "the crisis of contemporary life."

In the cyclical cosmology of the East, cosmic death and rebirth occurs repeatedly throughout eternity and is sometimes described metaphorically as the inspiration and exhalation of the Author of our being, Who forever breathes forth and withdraws the manifested universe. In the linear metaphysics of the West, death and rebirth occurs but once, at the end of time, and is called the Apocatastasis. In either case it is nothing to lament, being in the nature of things, and for those liberated souls who, conscious of their position in the descending trajectory of cosmic time, have achieved or been awarded the requisite spiritual detachment, this great moment, apparently a supreme calamity, is even the occasion for rejoicing, in that it heralds the recovery of aboribinal purity and the dawn of a new grace. A cosmic cycle is said to end when the being at its center, in this case humanity, has lost its spiritual knowledge.

Much of this exegesis was kindly imparted to me by Dr. Frank, who explained that there are also secondary levels of meaning in the evocation of the earthly paradise, symbolizing humanity's perpetual longing to return to the timeless bliss of Eden before the Fall, and in an implied analogy to the return to the "kingdom within," the repository of mankind's creative and renewing powers, on the part of the early Christian communities in the period of the decline of the Roman Empire. For these scattered seeds of the great civilization which would one day be called Western Christendom, the Empire, or the old order, was already dead and the new order was already born: the inner kingdom, "Life Eternal," was alone real. We are compelled to assume that in Sister Angela's eyes the entire modern world, in its crisis, corresponds to Rome, an assertion to which we can only respond, it would seem, and if we are to be candid, with a shrug. A perspective so vast as the one contained in this paper cannot be proven true or false; it can only be received and contemplated.

Despite her failing health, Sister Angela insisted upon reading her paper herself. She read it carefully and slowly, occasionally looking up at the audience with a radiant smile. There was no applause at the end. The entire assemblage rose to its feet, stood a moment in silent homage and then, still in silence, filed out of the room.

I made no entry in my journal that night, and I can recall the flash of amusement accompanying my realization that I couldn't tell whether I had broken my customary discipline because I had too much to say or because I had nothing to say at all.

Homage to Reality:
How It Looks To Those Who Can See It

by Sister Angela Prescott

Everything awaits them now at last, the real ocean, wave upon wave, and the sky, and the land, the inarticulate turf and sod, suppressed but invulnerable—now everything awaits them at last in the truth. Savage and glorious, the Earth flowers into victory. Never was love more vivid, more conscious of its sovereignty. Death is a mirror of birth, the end a mirror of the beginning, full circle a return to the source.

The cities, unmasked and prostrate, no longer boast the power to enchant their quest. If they dare to see, if they choose, they walk the streets exalted; with audacious elation they declare themselves whole again. The direct intuition of life, intact, perfect, as if the slow dissolution and long exile had been only a moment's distraction, a fitful dream, is reborn within them, rewarding its vindication with peace. Whatever may have happened, whatever rending tearing judgement may have shredded the world's coherence, the essences of things abide, eternal and inviolate, like stars, gleaming in constellations beyond the reach of sight or mind.

Once again, as in the beginning, the world faithfully astonishes their expectant appraisal. Once again nothing is real but the living moment. They inhabit the freshness of perpetual creation; a bird wheeling in the wind, the shifting gliding shadows of leaves gently lapping at the grass and clover, the diamonds of sunlight or fleeting smudges of color that dart through the lattice of shrubbery to startle their delight—all are more real than the centuries of history, the sheer crushing accumulated weight of irreversible time, the fabricated environments of numbers and facts in which their lives were smothered before they awoke to the truth. No;

124

not merely *more* real, but altogether real, alone real, as if
compared with a fiction, a nightmare, a mirage, or an error:
the sole fatal error to which such beings are prone. Before
their calm gaze, devoid of pity or irony or regret, in which no
trace of nostalgia or curiosity even lingers for a moment,
"the works of man" become exactly that, "the works of
man": who could ever have believed in them? How could
they possibly have merited the trust of their creators?

Rain rejoices, fire rejoices: their depths at last are sounded.
The watering of the cities is fruitless in all senses, and the
thwarted rain—the cold squalls gusting avidly across barren
rooftops, asphalt and cement in vain search of soil and seeds,
the coursing rivulets trapped inside a rigid maze of gutters,
pipes and sewers where germination is baffled by a sunless
wasteland of rust and sterile slime—invokes in their memories a counter-vision of the ancient Earth, in their hearts a
longing for true rainfall quenching the thirst of a true land,
and their longing is its longing, what actually happens is that
the rain longs for itself in their hearts, recovers itself in the
world of which they, reborn into reality, are the center. As it
was once a god, whose beneficence, conjured by dance or
prayer or faithful patience, was life itself, it becomes visible
again as a being, a presence, a law: a harbinger whose purpose cannot be defied, nor its bounty repulsed. The longing
for what has vanished is love of the essences—which means
love of God Who is their Source—and therefore the seed of
rebirth. Fire, also resurrected, is now again the devourer of
the worlds, the self-consumption of vainglorious vitality, the
inferno of decomposition into which all things upon their
consummation plummet: the hearth, fulfilled, becomes an
oracle. In the merciful respite of night, in the stillness where
both television and the hell from which it emanates have
been annihilated, the embers—the eternal embers, primordial, changeless and timeless, uncontaminated by drama or
history—release their final secret to the beings they taught
to brood upon the day's elusive import, to respect the hum-

ble inclinations of reverie, and to acknowledge in fulfillment
of their dignity an appropriate servitude to the laws and
manners of a world they never deserved. Now again, as in
the pure beginning, in the breathing on the waters, each
living thing is life itself—with a vengeance; each child is the
future—with a vengeance; and violence, beyond all shadow
of a doubt, is an earnest of the end—with a vengeance. The
world becomes its sanctities again. Sacrilege and holiness,
miracle and profanation, imbalance and proportion, now are
visible, tangible, undeniable. Violations of the nature of
things destroy those who perpetrate them, right or wrong,
rebel or tyrant: now it can be seen, now it is proven.

The fugitive definitions imposed by history are nothing to
them. They see things as they really are, in themselves, and
because they see things as they are the world relives creation
wherever they turn. They have surrendered their wills and
become the realm of bliss in which the world contemplates
itself. A martyr is a martyr now and a morning is a morning:
there are no nations and the days have no date. They bear
witness to the return of the archetypes, the immortals, and
they know their witness is providence. It's time to begin
anew.

Impassive but not aloof, the perfect solemnity of its self-
absorption—in the mountains etched by twilight or in the
tremor of a spider's web—neither diminished nor distracted
by their belated homage, equally indifferent to defiance and
contrition, the world receives as its own, as its knowledge of
itself, the banished virtues which they with solemn fervor
now embrace. They are home again. Once more austerity
illuminates the solitude of things, their fragile economy and
primeval excellence, and compassion answers to the great
dependence. As before in the golden age, in the garden faint
and painful no longer but thrilling now in their memories, so
again in the new beginning born of the courage to face the
end, humility and good will, truthfulness and harmlessness,
gratitude, serenity and the mystery of charity are the reflec-

tions upon Earth of the eternal reality in Heaven, guaranteeing by their obedient audience and response that the world will hold together, and by their recollection that it will be reborn. The virtues create the world: they believe it: they know it. In the darkness the age of darkness, an animated costumed corpse feverishly enacting a stream of delirious fantasies in vain hope of diverting the terrified suspicion that life has vanished, denounces itself now in every moment, naked before the remorseless reconnaissance of those in whose discernment it perished. Vulgarity and hypocrisy, banality, ugliness and perfidy, surrounding them everywhere, only testify to the integrity of the purposes they desecrate, as adulteration and perversion testify to the purity they defile.

They know they aren't human. They know they aren't individuals. As the cycle draws to a close, and the frenzy of denial called "daily life" reaches its crescendo, the spirit whose manifestation called itself human becomes again the Self it always was behind the great spectacle it sustains, the infinite peace glowing at the heart of Creation stands unveiled, and "humanity," in radiant submission to the Eternity from which it arises and to which it must return, realizes itself as a world whose time of death and rebirth is at last at hand. The transfiguration of all beings and things is at hand. Neither human nor separate, they are the presiding intelligence and true self-awareness within everything, and by which everything exists. They are a timeless world, suspended, among an infinity of other worlds, in the Mind of God, as their planet, that very world cast into time, hangs suspended in the boundless reaches of space, adrift among the galaxies and stars: in the night sky, in the celestial apparition called the heavens, whose beauty they adore and whose majesty they worship not in themselves now but as an augury, given in mercy, of the Beauty and Majesty from which they proceed, and of the Wisdom to which their world has now been summoned. They are at peace. When they regard their green Earth, the hills and meadows, the over-hanging trees, the wild ducks curving down to the still water, they see the garden again, the first and only garden, their place of peace. They respond to the will of God with the love of God.

The waves burst upon the mussel-studded rock. Wave upon wave, heave, fold, burst into spray and wash across the jagged stubborn rock, and then stream back, a fringe of foaming braids, into the gulping turbulence of dark water and green froth that encircles, like a hissing necklace, the stone throat thrust up from the ocean floor. They are not deceived. The grip of history, the grip of the dying order, has been broken. They know the rock they see before them is not the rock that rose dripping from the water ages ago. Like the unborn witness of sentience in which it subsists, the rock stands outside of time, and they, welcomed into their extinction, enter laughing because they know now that they were always there, immortal and free. Wave, burst, spray and flood, streaming foam, and again the anemones bob up through the falling overflow and the black rock emerges, glistening, into the hammer of the sun. Again and again, ever returning, always the same, one truth re-enacted, and they exult. Those who bow to time are devoured by it: those who surrender to the eternal live forever. The gulls swooping and crying, white against blue, the sand, a tawny slope flattening into the swirl of surf, the bleached wood, the shells and salt—this moment, this realm, this habitation is their own, and the goal of their quest. To see existence as a miracle, that is the answer, that is the divine presence, and the miracle of existence is seen only in the world's vision of itself: when the I vanishes the world becomes real, and reality, as the sages have agreed, is infinite joy. It is not they who delight in the waves: the waves delight in themselves. Here in this vision, now, at the end, they find a theme of the great rebirth—a glimpse, a promise, a proof that they have not been forsaken, that they are loved.

The center of their triumph is holiness. They know existence is holy and they know holiness must be adored: to default in this adoration is to lose touch with reality. When reverence disappears it takes everything else with it, leaving behind only empty shells idolized in the ferocious pursuit of the life they once contained. They pursue nothing. They live, they worship, they wait. While in the ghostly cities the interminable metallic voices, in an endless avalanche of staccato gibberish, jabber to the stupefied protagonists reports of the history they are making, at a speed so breathtaking the reporters can barely keep pace, and the age of darkness hurls itself toward oblivion in an accelerating bedlam of ceaseless activity, the noise level rising relentlessly to its deafening climax, they worship and they wait. The center of their triumph is holiness, the divine origin and presence which is salvation. The cities, like history, are nothing to them: antics and capers: the dance of death. It's all over, and they know it. They discriminate between the unreal and the real. They turn from death toward immortality, from darkness toward light.

Once more the integrity of things proclaims to their instinct of deference its primacy, once more they heed the claims of their world. Now again as before in the first bright days, wood, soil and stone yield their earnest admonitions to those who share the miracle, food, air and water announce their heavenly lineage and inherent purpose, and the pristine is articulate to their respect. The Earth is visibly a being, divine because it is perfect, perfect because it is divine, and once more—in their smile of praise, in their certitude, in their thankfulness, tranquillity and fascinated restraint— there circulates between mind and world the sacramental commerce by which the cosmos is redeemed.

The children sleep out on the meadow under the stars, ringed by the murmur of the night breeze in the laurel, embraced by the inconceivable consciousness in which the galaxies blaze and their dreams unfold. Beyond the silhouetted coastal range moonlit waves, born of winds a thousand miles out at sea, burst on the black mussel-studded rocks jutting up through the dark sand, then sigh back to join the next surge, returning in joy forever. On the side of the planet facing the sun, bathed with the life-giving light, the leaf-shadows quiver on the quivering grass, ants file down the clover stems, and wild geese, emerging from the over-hanging branches trailing their tips in the water, paddle toward the center of the shimmering noonday pond, criss-crossing the slow ripples of each other's wakes. They who have turned their backs on history are at peace with the world. Creation awaits them. Breathless, humming with bees, the garden they remember once again awaits them. They are real. What they have made of themselves has died, what God has made of them alone remains. Once again they are His children, the immortal birth.

They know that it is only because the world is beautiful that it is real. They know that the Earth *is* the love of the Earth. They know that to believe in the age of darkness is to cease to exist. They know that joy is union with reality, and that to decipher reality—the mystery of conscious presence, the mystery of their being, the miracle of a world—is their task at the end. They are the knowledge that is not learned but realized: they are the axioms that orient, the truths that save.

They love to pray. They love to sit cross-legged on the ground, out of doors, under the sky, and pray. Their longing to pray is the world's longing to be hallowed, to know itself in God: this truth is revealed to them in prayer itself. So they accept the gift as it is given and offer it back to the God who gave it, knowing that the acceptance and the offering, the world, the prayer and the being who prays, are all one, that all distinctions vanish in the divine Oneness. Enlightenment is the world, the surrender to God is freedom: so long as they can love, all is well. The will of God is the nature of things: the truth is submission. In Spring the fine weather invites happiness and lightens the heart, the air softens, and warm light, casting blurred shadows through the overhanging branches, glows translucent in the reeds swaying at the water's edge. The rains return to bless the garden, the morning dew sparkles on the spider webs trembling in the fragrant grass. There is no death. They live and love by the unfailing grace of God. Beatitude awaits them, now and as always. The end, confronted with faith, announces the beginning, ever returning and always the same, one truth re-enacted, and they are the immortal Witness, pure bliss and infinite peace, in which the Great Wheel turns forever. The world is a promise that will be kept.

The Eye of the Heart:
A Fable

Introduction

Pierre Flynn received his Ph.D in Anthropology from Rutgers University in 1954 and did graduate research in the history of religions at the Sorbonne and at the University of Glasgow. Born in 1925, he is the author of numerous studies in oriental mythology and shamanism; he is currently on the faculty of the University of Chicago.

His was the only comic paper presented to the Conference. It is a satire from beginning to end, written, of course, with deadly serious intent and, I would say, with deadly accuracy as well. His perspective, both on people and on the crisis of contemporary life, is religious and the target of his kindly multi-layered irony is unregenerate human nature. Unless we can be persuaded to love and heed the truth, he argues, and to subordinate the aggressive appetites of the ego, both on an individual and an international scale, to the empathetic and all-inclusive vision of "the eye of the heart," we are doomed.

His statement, however, is contained much more in his literary style—which reminded me a bit of Thorstein Veblen's—than in any theoretical position one might seek to extract from his hilariously intricate prose. He presents us more with a sensibility than an analysis, a sensibility which, observing human nature both from a religious vantage point and with the irony of mature disillusion, responds to the disconcerting tableau with mingled dismay and compassion, and, I am afraid, little hope. Oddly enough, however, it is that "little hope," at least so it seemed to me, which seems to linger after the laughter subsides. Certainly Dr. Flynn is burdened with no misconceptions about the potential for evil in human nature, which in his view is rooted principally in the fatal and willful blindness of egoism: equally certainly, however, he believes in our fundamental and indestructible potential for good, which derives from our power to see and love the truth, this potential having been placed within us by the "First Principle" Himself. In what proportions we display these potentials is our choice alone, and, he suggests, our seemingly incorrigible predilection for the darker option, and our corresponding hostility to the truth, to those who confront us with it and even to our own intuition of it, is the theme of human history, the inner dynamic of our daily lives, and the root of the present crisis.

In terms of its scholarship, Dr. Flynn's paper, I am told, is fairly riddled with allusions to the doctrines and episodes of the five major world religions, and its central category, "the eye of the heart," appears, in precisely those words, in all five of their mystical traditions. The import of these allusions, however, is sufficiently and deliberately generalized in the text, and while a familiarity with religious literature will perhaps render certain passages more amusing, it is by no means necessary to a full appreciation of the paper.

The position of Dr. Flynn's contribution as the last in this book is purely accidental, in that the papers, as I mentioned in the Introduction, and for the reason stated there, are presented in the order in which I heard them at the Conference. There is, however, a certain finality about it, in my opinion, in that without losing the totality provided only by religious perspectives it yet manages to retrieve the spiritual drama from the superhuman implacable vastnesses of the cosmic process, where Sister Angela perceived it with such lucid faith, and bring it down to earth, into our daily lives, into the human heart itself. It is there, we have often been assured, that our true hope dwells.

A stocky rather dapper-looking man, Dr. Flynn delivered his paper with obvious relish, and upon a few occasions, to everyone's added delight, actually broke down and laughed aloud. There is, however, an element of extremity or desperation in the satirical approach which, I am quite certain, was neither lost upon the audience nor peripheral to Dr. Flynn's inspiration: his paper, after all, was written for a Conference whose theme was crisis. The comic relief provided by satire is perhaps necessitated by its refusal to underestimate.

Dr. Flynn's was the nineteenth paper delivered and occasioned the following, and final, entry in my journal.

Our lives, it would appear, are destined unfailingly to astonish us. It may be that, in Dr. Rosenblatt's universal and perhaps overstated drama, I have taken a few steps toward "the boundary" here at Sandstone. But the ground is still firm beneath my feet. One reaches a time in one's life—I think Pierre Flynn has reached it: he reminds me of myself in many ways—where it becomes clear that an increasing detachment from insignificance lies ahead, where the power to discriminate has been fairly well acquired. Growth must assume different forms in the different stages of one's journey; it becomes, with the years, less wild, involuntary and impetuous, more discerning, more accurate, more consistent with itself. If the impulse toward "the boundary" is like wind, we learn to tack our sails.

It could be argued with equal cogency that Dr. Flynn's paper is passionately engaged and utterly detached. Perhaps that's the trick of wisdom, the elusive solution: external engagement, internal detachment. Easy enough to evoke it through literary artifice—quite another thing to sustain it in one's person. Dr. Harrison's engagement, on the other hand, his uncritical love of humanity, would seem to be inner as well as outer; perhaps he is pure: certainly his perspective falls within the modern "tradition" of revolution that has set countless noble minds, and the world, on fire. Or perhaps, as I speculated earlier in these pages, he is naive.

When all is said and done, it is the depth at which we live our lives that alone counts. That is the true measure. I have not been indifferent to depth; but I have felt that the matter was settled in my life, and there I was mistaken. (Perhaps it is never settled. Perhaps we have to be willing to sacrifice everything if we would know the final answer to our lives. Certainly, that has been the teaching.) It seems that I have been readying myself, all along and behind the scenes, for a deeper foray into myself, and out into the great world—an apparently simultaneous adventure. One can only submit.

This will be the last entry in my Sandstone journal. Summations are facile; I am no longer sentimental. Nothing is really ended till we die, and even then . . . I'll be leaving tomorrow evening, perhaps late. I hope there's no fog on the coast.

The Eye of the Heart:
A Fable

by Pierre Flynn

When the First Principle first thought of people, which for Him amounted to creating them, He gave them, as a gift to which their gratitude has never quite been equal, to say the least, a secret divine power, a power to see things with clarity both from the inside as they see themselves and from the outside in their place in the big picture, to help them recover their bearings and regain the true path when they went astray, as they certainly would, given their chronic penchant, despite the painful regret which invariably follows, to become enthusiastic or sentimental about things, imaginative or ambitious in their enterprises, or simply confused by their own conclusions, their penchant, in other words, to lose contact with reality, and this power of vision, which, unfortunately, functions with steadfast precision only for people, not exactly the run of the mill, but not necessarily saints either, who are generous, disciplined, appreciative, detached and compassionate, or simply sincere, sincerity being the mother of all virtues—this secret, somewhat unruly, alternately celebrated and despised, absolutely essential yet uncannily disturbing power of vision is called the Eye of the Heart.

Now the Eye of the Heart—which, for those who haven't caught on, is the Eye that sees the truth—just like the eyes of the head, can be either open or closed, keen or weak, clear or clouded, depending on the individual and the circumstances, although it has been known on occassion to snap open without warning and then shut again almost immediately, leaving its owner both bewildered and dismayed, and throughout that great adventure, called human history, which has brought so much laughter and so many tears to so many people, so much merriment and so much woe, the Eye of the Heart has played a major role, not so much, unfortunately, in the guidance it provided as in the sorry consequences of its neglect. Few would dispute that most of the time it was closed altogether, and that in those rare moments when it was open, and the seer, often the most ordinary of people, eagerly reported what it had revealed, the report was either bitterly contested or completely ignored, sometimes even ridiculed, and all too frequently, sadly enough, the dazzled seer had to wheel and run for cover. This happened so often in the course of time, as a matter of fact, and was observed through narrowed eyes by so many other potential seers whose Eye of the Heart had also been open, that "keeping your big mouth shut" eventully evolved into a widely accepted principle of self-preservation, and many people whose Eye of the Heart remained stubbornly open, or popped open unexpectedly, concluded that their talent must have been intended as a private diversion, and, when the vision was given, simply exchanged uneasy glances with their fellow citizens and held their tongues, or mumbled vague excuses and quietly slipped away from the scene of the action.

But history—fortunately, from one point of view—is only a tiny fraction of the human story; most of what has happened, almost all, indeed, had nothing to do with the great drama of war and peace, progress and regress, conquest and reversal, guile and gullibility, elation and disillusion, celebration and remorse, etiquette and mayhem, about which the lettered and the unlettered have been debating, sometimes quite violently, ever since it began. Most of what has happened was just plain people living the daily round, getting on by hook or by crook, eating, sleeping, loving, quarreling, singing, working and raising the children. And there, too, in those warmer more manageable worlds, the Eye of the Heart was either open or closed, keen or weak, clear or clouded.

The relationships between humanity and its Eye of the Heart, as well we might imagine, have been ambiguous, at best inconclusive. In the breasts of many people, especially those whose piety is impregnable, the realities revealed by the Eye of the Heart actually awaken sorrow, a sorrow sometimes amounting to loathing, which often masks itself, in public, as delicate regret; things are not what they ought to be. To others, these realities are merely amusing, and often confirm a suspicion, harbored without malice, even with a certain wry pity, that things are seldom what they appear to be. Responses to the revelations of the Eye of the Heart, indeed, may range from outrage to exhilaration, reverence to nausea, cheers to suicide, although it must be confessed that, considering the decreasing frequency, in this tragic era, with which the Eye of the Heart is opened at all, these responses are mainly a matter of cherished memory rather than living experience. The Eye of the Heart, some people say, is on the verge of closing for good, which would abandon the world to a fascinating chaos whose relief, swift or delayed, could only come about by catastrophe. But nothing is certain. The First Principle, at least such has been our faith, does not recall His gifts.

In children the Eye of the Heart is tightly shut. Although they are spontaneous, and by definition innocent, it must be admitted that neither spontaneity nor innocence, despite their charm, have proven reliable instruments in humanity's somewhat casual quest for the truth of its situation—at least since the Fall. The faint smile on the face of the world demands for its successful interpretation a greater, and more alarming, accumulation of undeserved suffering than people generally anticipate, a quantity rarely attained before the fifth decade of life, and, as many will have surmised, suffering, in all it exotic variety, is a great stimulus, but by no means a sufficient one, to the opening of the Eye of the Heart. Amazingly enough—but not so amazing in the view of those who have wearied, to the breaking point, of the endless charade to which we are all subjected—suffering can also have quite the opposite effect, that of shutting the Eye of the Heart if not permanently, at least with a settled, grim or even ferocious resolve; nor must we condemn those who have been so harshly and inadvertently penalized by the incomprehensible ordinances of nature: it is the First Principle, we must recall, Who casts the first stone, and, we might add, for Whom all things are possible. There are many, and their reasons are many, in whom the Eye of the Heart rarely if ever opens, but none, we are compelled to believe, in whom the closure is irreversible.

But however that may be, whatever Providence may intend, our hopes must not be dimmed. The point of this narration—can it be that I have neglected to mention it altogether?—is to suggest that only a nearly universal opening of the Eye of the Heart, improbable as such a thorough reversal of trends may sound, can rescue humanity from the wretched fate it so single-mindedly pursues, and it is with that unlikely but perhaps not impossible resolution in view that I propose an anatomy, as it were, of the Eye, to further our deeper understanding of its methods and powers, its friends and, for we must be truthful here, its enemies.

We have already noted people's mixed reactions to the revelations of the Eye of the Heart, and the resulting prudent circumspection in the breasts of those to whom the vision is granted. It might be well, at this point, to examine more narrowly the various character types who dance the suspicious minuet in which seer and audience confront each other's appraisal.

More often than not, the inner truth or overview revealed to the Eye of the Heart urges, rather than an expansion or intensification of effort, a halt, often immediate, to the strenuous undertakings of which most people are so fond, or at least a pause for reassessment. To the man or woman of action, naturally, such a proposal can only be received as an irksome or even insulting intrusion, an addle-brained if not sinister invitation to irresponsibility. "Wait and see," "Leave well enough alone," "Let sleeping dogs lie," and "Flow with it" express attitiudes which jar unpleasantly with the diligent vigor of those who labor to improve their lot, or the selfless fury of those who labor to improve the world. The polite arguments offered in defense of this vision often seem to proceed from squeamishness, cowardice or sheer indolence, even stupidity, and the insights they claim, which seem to suggest, incredibly enough, that the world should be left as it is, or, by logical implication and even worse, that it should have been left as it was, rarely fail to anger or exasperate the impatient audience glaring, as it were, from the pits and bulwarks whose industrious excavation the timid seer so inanely interrupted.

But the affairs of the Eye of the Heart are never elementary, never obvious. Their essence, indeed, is a paradox. It is simply not true, as many well-meaning people aver, that the Eye of the Heart counsels a withdrawal into passivity in all circumstances; the poignant relationship between seer and audience just described is often reversed, especially upon occasions destined for notoriety or renown, and the invariably unwelcome seer, when all is said and done, is really quite as likely to startle the complacency of his or her listeners with a peremptory demand that action be initiated as he or she is to vex their fervor with a proposal that it be renounced. (Can it be that there is something innately recalcitrant in human nature which resists, by its very essence, vehemently, obstinately, even savagely, the vision of the Eye of the Heart? Is there another vision, another point of view, another interpreter of events residing within us, devoid of empathy and indifferent, even hostile, to harmony, which claims with implacable jealousy its right to guide our destinies? But I digress.) It is the unfamiliar, almost weird, even, repugnant course of action encouraged by the Eye of the Heart which elicits the fierce but misguided accusation of fatalism. The Eye of the Heart, at least such appears to have been the intention of its Fashioner, devotes its scrutiny to the latent peace and harmony within things, too hastily over-looked in these headlong times, and strives to illuminate the path, of whose very existence or even merit so many people are skeptical, that leads back from uproar to equilibrium, from excitement to peace of mind, from exertion to effortlessness; the action it encourages, in other words, although quite real, is likely to seem a retreat rather than an advance, to seem lacking in the appropriate nobility, lacking in audacity, high aspiration or appropritate magnitude, lacking even in purpose, to seem, in a word, humble. Such, however, is its nature and defense, as well as the explanation—or excuse, if one be required—for the cryptic and perhaps equivocal observations of those in whose innocent souls the Eye of the Heart is open.

But let us recall, in anticipation of an argument the careful reader may be formulating, that the Eye of the Heart is in reality the possession and in potential the living vision of everyone. It is not limited to a rash handful sentenced to loneliness, misunderstanding and contempt, if not worse, in their confrontation with a suspicious audience comprising the majority of the commonwealth. Although such confrontations have certainly shaken society at large for thousands of years, where they usually, as it were, "made the headlines," and although they compose the true substance, the true encounter beneath the artful surface, of countless moments in people's daily lives, the confrontation between seer and audience, in its most dramatic purity—without costume, as it were—occurs within the individual. This is a very important point. The earnest inner debate between the Eye of the Heart and what might be called, by contrast, the Blindness, is the real cause of much of the inexplicable human behavior which perplexes our curiosity and baffles our acumen. It explains why people, even the most detached among us, are so prone to lash out at loved ones suddenly and without warning; why we giggle at the wrong times;

why we turn sheepish and offer lame apologies, or refuse to offer anything, out of respect for our dignity, and then suffer irritating remorse; why we rant, bluster and denounce, and then with solemn penitance recant; why we become mysteriously adamant, mysteriously evasive, mysteriously docile or mysteriously glum; why we feign gruffness when we feel tenderness, and tenderness when we feel nothing. The explanation is the inner debate, so stubbornly prolonged and so fatefully ignored, between the Eye of the Heart and the Blindness, of which the outer debate, the depressing encounter between reluctant seer and suspicious audience, is but the shadow. The inner world—scarcely noticed, much less accorded priority, in the welter of creativity into which so many today have cast their hope—was actually deemed of great significance, and even greater consequence, by the First Principle, although, it must be admitted in fairness to both sides, many of His official representatives consider this perspective, perhaps legitimate at one time, to have been rendered obsolete by the pace and direction of events.

In daily life, as it is called, the Eye of the Heart opens wide in amazement, narrows inquisitively or with secret satisfaction, stares with profound disillusion, glares with unwavering conviction, squints with mistrust, glances with amusement or detachment, peeks with thrilled curiosity, gazes with serene assurance, gapes in disbelief, snaps shut in alarm and even bats fatuously. It's very busy, totally "into it" as the vivid expression goes; strictly speaking, it can never be said to sleep. Factory and office workers, for example, whose vision is sharper and more alert than many people suspect, see quite clearly, and with continuous reconfirmation of their conclusion, that factories and offices are the result of a grave error committed at some unknown time in the past by persons equally unknown; so, it would appear, are many other restlessly tolerated social institutions. There is in factory and office workers, as a matter of fact, a sort of constant poignant peering by the Eye of the Heart, as if through bars, a discontent much noted, but invariably misinterpreted, by their ideological champions, in whom, oddly enough, the Eye of the Heart generally suffers from a rare form of tunnel vision. It is almost painfully agape, on the contrary, in conscientious teachers questioning immigrant parents about their children's abilities, in bus drivers waiting for a red light at urban intersections after dark, in sensitive teen-agers listening to political speeches on television, and in men and women gloomily relieving themselves in their own bathrooms at the end of the day; it is tightly shut, on the other hand, in people experiencing rage or fervor, lust or avarice, euphoria or despair or any of the other vices or extremes; and it is blurred in almost everyone almost all the time.

For reasons already made abundantly clear, the Eye of the Heart, except in instances of uncontrollable impulse or elaborate precaution, keeps its own counsel. And this prohibition of an intelligence crying to be articulate does not go without its consequences for the human vessel by whose firm discretion the vision is stifled. The prudent seer can often be seen muttering under his or her breath, flashing enigmatic smiles on inappropriate occasions, or ostentatiously wiping away a vagrant tear. To see the truth and keep silent, while undoubtedly advisable, is a strain upon the compulsion to communicate which seems inseparable, unfortunately, from the vision granted to the beleaguered recipient of insight. The numerous styles of mature reserve with which adults confront the taxing challenges of daily life, often hastily misinterpreted as lethargy, arrogance, stupidity or suppressed hysteria, are products of this very strain.

It is certainly true that those in whom the Eye of the Heart is generally open are rarely successful by worldly standards, at least not for very long, no matter how abhorrent this assertion may sound to defenders of the official mythology.

The vision that sees from within, moved by empathy, or from without, in quest of harmony, has proven singularly unsuccessful in perceiving its own advantage, or even, indeed, in grasping what its own advantage might be—a dilemma happily resolved by the First Principle in His scheme to make the last first and the first last. The seer is often lax or maladroit in financial matters, deaf to the knocking of opportunity, loath to take initiative on his or her own behalf, and incompetent in distinguishing powerful allies from powerless nobodies. This awkward, almost laughable social performance, with its resulting embarrassment in social status, may be seen as yet further evidence of the uneasy relationship between the Eye of the Heart and the commonwealth whose security, and indeed survival, it was meant to guarantee. This is not to say, however, by any means, that habitual closure of the Eye of the Heart is indispensable to individual advancement or to the assumption of public responsibility, nor to suggest that—if I may borrow a phrase pungent with the bluff vulgarity of the vernacular—"the scum always rises to the top." The Eye of the Heart, when all is said and done, has a life of its own which is independent of external circumstances; it may be, contrary to the axiom of dogmatists, wide open in the so-called successful, and simply ignored, or, contrary to the prejudice of sentimentalists, tightly shut in the downtrodden. The ways of the First Principle, to the consternation of some and the relief of others, are not our own.

There are people who, due to the mysterious workings of their Eye of the Heart—mysterious, as the reader will recall, are His ways—occupy a sort of ambiguous troubled middle station in life. In this class of people, often annoyingly hampered by guilt and disdain at the same time, the Eye of the Heart has managed to foil supervision, as it occasionally does, and has diluted with insight, before its possessors realized what was happening, the otherwise pure ferocity of their worldly ambitions. In a word, they were compelled to see beyond the circle of their own concerns, and were subtly handicapped by a draining of resolve, by a deepening of intuition, in the midst of the universal rivalry to which everyone, on pain of death, is implacably summoned. More people are victims of this discouraging accidental side effect of the Eye of the Heart's wakefulness than is commonly supposed. To accuse the Eye of deliberate cunning, however, would be, of course, absurd, and those afflicted with a vision that interferes with the pursuit of their chosen goals usually attribute their misfortune to the unfathomable design of those unidentified cosmic personalities whose deafness to the just protests of their victims is proverbial. But inwardly they are troubled by a gnawing doubt, as are so many to whom a partial vision is granted, and to such a degree that many people in this peculiar amorphous category are driven to seek the counsel of professional sages, although, as if to add a crowning irony to the labyrinth of their lives, more often than not the sages from whom they seek illumination languish in a darkness deeper than that of their consultants.

It may by this point have struck the reader that an examination of life and people in terms of their relationship to the First Principle's gift of vision is somewhat depressing. To an extent, of course, this is true, as indeed the sorry plight of a humanity deprived of divine vision, and the destruction by inadvertent suicide toward which their world in this deprivation would inevitably plummet, was the very reason for which the First Principle, in His mercy, gave us the gift in the First Place. But "depressing" is as good a word as any, and in response we can only point out that to seek encouragement elsewhere would be futile. There is nothing else; and, although to many this assertion may sound horrifying, if not sacrilegious, there never was. The Eye of the Heart—or, if precision be the reader's fetish, the mercy of the First Principle—alone can save us. Nor must we abandon hope; for although it is unquestionably the Blindness from which humanity in general at present seeks guidance, there are a growing number who, as it were, scratch their heads, and dare to wonder.

The foregoing observations cannot but summon to mind once again the burring question of humanity's immediate collective destiny, nor fail to reawaken those misgivivings concerning the competence, indeed the sanity, of planetary leadership with which so many people are tormented. For it is here that Providence has challenged our cleverness with one of its most ingenious paradoxes, the paradox that those in whom a wide open Eye of the Heart is most necessary and would be most beneficial, humanity's helmspersons, are so often those in whom it is most obstinately shut. True, it is by collective sufferance—in all meanings of the term—that a position of leadership is acquired and maintained; but this peculiar sanction, if anything, serves rather to heighten the paradox than to mitigate it, and our intelligence is left even more helpless than it was before. Some would argue that, in the final analysis, humanity must find its consolation in the fact that divine paradoxes are inherent, almost rampant, in the plan of the First Principle and are by definition beyond human comprehension, and are therefore responsive to pious faith rather than impudent interrogation; others, with equal cogency and perhaps a trace of scorn, would retort that those scoundrels whom the commonwealth in haste has elevated may with equivalent dispatch be junked, and that an appeal to Providence in these instances, however sincere, can only serve to prolong, and indeed unwittingly apologize for, the indignity of mismanagement in public life. We have here, however, entered the realm of political debate, a realm from which the wise quietly withdraw, murmuring whatever excuses might be most acceptable to the glaring antagonists, whose jealously guarded differences are, at least from their own point of view, the sole support of the modern world. Whether the blindness of leadership be a paradox of Providence or an infamy the commitment to justice cannot tolerate, the Eye of the Heart, it must be insisted, not unlike light itself, is merely a witness, not a partisan, a revealer, not an interpreter, and by its nature sympathetic to all; and it is precisely the stupefied or enraged, crafty or contemptuous reception with which this approach is greeted that explains why so many of the naive seers who rushed headlong with true vision into the scandal of public affairs rarely did so a second time.

But we have strayed from the warm tangible human world in which the Eye of the Heart is at home, the world of living people in their earthly setting where eyes both of the head and the heart have always found their feast, and their task, into the wintry arid world of theory and controversy where the Eye of the Heart can descry nothing, perhaps because, although many will spring to their feet with indignation at the suggestion, there is nothing there. Let us return then to the real field of action, to daily life. For most people, upon whose shoulders the privilege of participation in history has weighed rather more heavily than expected, this realm, this simple daily life, a land, a home and a family, a village or a tribe, has been all they ever had or needed or wanted—a testimony perhaps to the intractable smallmindedness of the human race—as their patient, trudging perpetual return from the wars as soon as conscription is rescinded, or their headlong flight as soon as surveillance is relaxed (if not sooner), have abundantly demonstrated.

The Eye of The Heart, as we have discovered, —I insert a brief summary at this point—is the common property of everyone, a gift of the First Principle which, while too much neglected to have ever actually been abused, has, by the same token, rarely been appreciated at its true worth. It sees with clarity both those great truths which when left unuttered abandon humanity to misery and despair, and when uttered are—most of the time but not always— misunderstood or abominated. And the thesis of this narration is that precisely in that narrow margin, that "but not always," lies our only hope for a fresh beginning. ("Why hope at all?" people cry recklessly or ironically, roguishly or angrily, despondently or pointedly—to which the answer, adverb for adverb, must be "Why ask the question?") Let us, then, resume our exploration whose nobility of purpose, and stark necessity, alone redeem it from the emptiness of idle twaddle, pathetic self-deception or madness.

In the haven of the domestic circle, where the Eye of the Heart is plagued by an insensitivity to its insights whose volcanic brutality can only be suggested, if at all, by comic-strip caricatures of neanderthal life, the seer encounters some of his or her bitterest repudiations. Few spouses fail to fall into surly or contemptuous silence in response to the snarls and jeers with which their insights are, as it were, clubbed to the ground, and, over the years, the great major-ity, in the absence of sympathetic communion, simply resign themselves, when evasion is unsuccessful, to the wiles and stratagems to which the character of their antagonist is most vulnerable. There are moments, of course, even whole days; but that the Eye of the Heart fares poorly in family life can scarcely be contested. It even seems at times, and in verification of the seer's most enraging suspicion, as if the content of the vision is irrelevant, and that it is the seer himself or herself, not the vision, which is the object of loathing.

It has been speculated, even at times argued with great heat, that the vision of the Eye of the Heart is incommunica-ble, a possibility which, even on the basis of the scanty and somewhat haphazard evidence adduced in this narration, cannot be discounted. The reason for this incommunicabil-ity, it is argued, is that the vision of the Eye of the Heart induces in the seer a state of, as it were, exaltation, and that unless this state is somehow transmitted to the audience, or at least perceived and respected—a triumph which, with the exception of a handful of notable sermons and addresses, has proven beyond the reach of mere mortals—the content of the vision loses most if not all of its persuasive power, and the excited seer is either pitied as a crackpot or detained as a troublemaker.

Others argue, however, that the incommunicability of this vision is exaggerated. The defenders of this more hopeful opinion assert that the sharing of exaltation, while certainly not commonplace, especially in these distressingly prosaic times, is in its travesty nearly universal, and only awaits the proper stimulus or occasion to revert to its authentic mode. This is a powerful argument, although its scrupulous elaboration might lead to hidden pitfalls. A third point of view, by far the most common, pooh-poohs the necessity and indeed the reality of exaltation altogether, claiming that strict adherence to the relevant facts, appropriate strategy and organizational discipline are all that is needed to promulgate visions of the truth, whatever their source and whatever their goal. This diversity of views, it would seem, only further demonstrates the ambivalence of humanity's relationship to the gift of divine vision, and although this ambivalence may justly be regarded as disheartening, the fierceness with which the various views are defended may with equal justice be welcomed as encouraging. The Eye of the Heart challenges our ultimate resources.

But the issue of the communicability of the vision—brought to the fore, as the reader will recall, by our sobering observations on the fate of the Eye of the Heart in the arena of domestic relations—is a crucial one and merits further examination. It is possible that direct sharing of vision—heart to heart, as it were—is restricted to privileged moments, either of intimacy or great peril, when the barriers of pride or shame are broken down under the pressure of circumstances. It is possible, in other words, that the vision given by the Eye of the Heart is more readily offered and more warmly received in the privacy of the bedroom or the lifeboat than in more mundane settings: that our encounters with the great realities of Love and Death tend to burn off, as it were, the thick layers of artifice and posture with

which the truth is customarily encrusted. What is required
in the present crisis, then, if the Eye of the Heart is to be
opened and its saving vision shared by multitudes, would be
a sense that love and death actually are issues of contemporary concern. The awakening of such a sense, while undoubtedly improbable at present due to the bewitching, almost
stupefying array of distractions with which we have, as it
were, decorated the inferno, would, on the other hand, tend
to become less so as the crisis deepens and the deities in
question force their twin presence more vividly upon the
public mind.

The role of the seer, in a sense, is analagous to the role of
the subordinate. Let us review a familiar scenario: the eager
subordinate—in a factory, a laboratory, an institution of
learning, a bureaucracy, an office, a political party or religious organization, a gambling syndicate or trade union or
athletic team: any hierarchical enterprise—reports to his or
her superior with an idea about how something might be
accomplished more efficiently or with greater prospect of
success; the superior, in the attitude of condescension—
polite or scoffing, sneering or curt or sly or smug—
approprite to the social status of the particular enterprise,
humors with lies the subordinate's impertinence or dis-
misses him or her outright; the subordinate, crestfallen or
embittered, returns to the interrupted task. The superior,
who might actually have already thought of the bright idea
on his or her own, or at least appreciated its merit during the
interview, knows full well the complex reasons, rooted in
greed and fear, why this particular idea must never be
brought into practice or even mentioned to certain people,
and also knows that the subordinate, who should have had
the good sense to keep quiet about it, is now a possible
source of trouble and, if he or she insists on being talkative
about the matter, will have to be silenced or terminated. It is
often with similar innocence and good will that the visions
of the Eye of the Heart are reported, and with similar acuity

that their broader implications are deciphered.

It cannot be denied that a great deal of what is very real and compelling, even momentous, to the eyes of the head is unreal, or at least merely symbolic, to the Eye of the Heart. This disparity is a principal source of confusion to those who inquire about the Eye, and, indeed, a principal impediment to the communication of its vision. Humanity's seers—which means, in potential, everyone, as I shall never tire of insisting—are frequently embarrassed by their inability to substantiate with solid facts and figures the truths of which they are nonetheless so certain, and all too often their plea is ignored and they themselves are made laughingstocks, stammering and protesting to no avail, not because of manifest or gross error, but simply because their arguments are deficient in that tangible proof which practical people invariably demand. How can we be certain, for example, that sincerity is a good thing and hypocrisy a bad thing, or that power corrupts? Unfortunately for the reputation of the Eye of the Heart, the truths it claims to reveal tend to be, as in the first example just cited, rather vague and over-generalized, or, as in the second example, outright cryptic. By the same token, the certainties in which the eyes of the head find comfort, and which constitute, indeed, the very foundations of our world—as, for example, "water boils at 212 degrees fahrenheit," or "the President's State of the Union message was interupted 22 times by wild applause," or "drug deaths won't keep Hollywood noses clean"—yet seem, in their aggregate, and despite the obvious ease with which they could be verified, to compose a world or a reality in which the wise might be reluctant to place their whole-hearted faith. It is almost as if, contrary to the evidence of the senses, the First Principle established two separate yet mysteriously interpenetrating orders of existence, one corresponding to the eyes of the head and the other to the Eye of the Heart.

It should be obvious by now that a chief function of the

Eye of the Heart, and a sufficient explanation for the unen-
thusiastic reception of its insights, is the ruffling of complacency. The magnitude of complacency, indeed, seems to vary
directly with the depth of the error, or the distance people
have strayed from the true path, which explains why the
truly thoroughgoing reprimands of humanity's seers,
responding to truly thoroughgoing deviations from the
path, have precipitated not only massive outbreaks of
hypocrisy, but an outrage and alarm at times approaching
panic. It is almost safe to say that wherever complacency is
irattled, be it by tearful outburst, penetrating criticism or
blistering denunciation, the Eye of the Heart has been
prompting a human vessel into speech, and many of the
really trenchant observations of the First Principle, either
delivered in Person or on His behalf, seem to have been
aimed at insidious complacency.

The careful reader, by this time, will be "getting the idea."
The Eye of the Heart, indifferent to the appearances which
most people find so enchanting, so intriguing, unimpressed
by status, reputation, custom, popularity or zeal, pierces
through the universal derangement to the inner truth of
things, to reality, while at the same time, being sublimely
impartial and identifying with no one's private hope, not
even the seer's, it ranges over the whole soul-stirring pano-
rama, the "big picture" within which all beings and things
discover their proper place and purpose, infallibly detecting
those presumptions and usurpations, those discords and
imbalances, invariably of human origin, which mar the
beauty and disfigure the perfection the First Principle had in
Mind. Could this divine vison be more frequently consulted
how happy we might be! To live the truth, to love only the
truth: that must be bliss! But alas, and as we have seen, such
is not the case. The external view, the partisan perspecive,
dominate. The inner light, undimmed but unheeded, con-
soles itself as it may.

The seers, in their social presence, may be divided into

four categories—loosely of course, since relations between the Eye of the Heart and its human recepticles are as notoriously unstable as their joint decisions are unpredictable. Let us now, with a view to summarizing our somewhat meandering observations, and before proceding to their conclusion, examine these general categories and explore with more insistent inquiry, to their very depths, if possible, the inner drama and its outward consequence, the revealing moments and poignant episodes, in which the Eye of the Heart plays its forever hopeful and forever aborted role. Our task in this narration is to make absolutely clear, so at least no one may appeal to their ignorance, the necessity and intention of the divine gift, its unalterable incompatibility with the quest for personal satisfaction, and its fateful place in the future we all face with such anguished hope and hopeless anguish.

There are, saddest and most common of all, the seers who, having been squelched or ignored beyond endurance, have fallen into a permanent silence, usually sullen or inscrutable but occasionally mischievous, as if perpetually hinting, with nervous winks and glances quickly suppressed by a twinge of prudence, that more lies here than meets the eye. In this category are serious men never taken seriously, usually due to some irrelevant flaw in their biographies, and thoughtful women never conceded the power of thought, due to the even more irrelevant accident of gender. These people are always thinking, "But of course nobody ever listens to *me!*"

Then there are that brave company we may call the manipulating seers, those who, having despaired of being straightfoward but refused nonetheless to surrender, resort instead to flattery and artifice, as if the human race were basically childlike and incapable of grasping its own true interests, and therefore both demanded and deserved to be beguiled. Many people, at one time or another, have been attracted by the role of the manipulating seer, and this solution, to which the Eye of the Heart has, as it were, stooped, has been perhaps its most successful strategem. The effectiveness of a manipulating seer, of course, will be in direct proportion to his or her anonymity, so the greatest among them, paradoxically enough, will slumber forever in unmarked graves, and their contribution to our salvation remain inaccessible to measurement. We may suspect, however, whether with irony or humility, that the demands made upon the ingenuity of manipulating seers will be more taxing in the future than they have been in the past, and we can only pray that the fertility of their invention and the cunning of their devices will be equal to the momentous occasion to which we have referred several times in this narration. Nor must we be angered or repelled by the spectacle of a being whose only alternative to self-destruction is self-deception, since it is altogether possible that our survival to the present has depended fully as much upon self-deception as may our survival in the future, and if this is the case we are clearly forced to admit, bowing, as we must, before the self-validating magnificence of humanity's achievements, that the fruit of the manipulating seers' devoted subterranean enterprise—the centuries of patient wheedling, coaxing and conniving, the countless moments of doubt, despair and self-hatred—fully vindicates their unsung sacrifice.

The stubborn seers, a hardy thick-skinned breed, few in number but always large in presence, simply refuse to be discomfited or ignored. Although often vilified as simpletons, perverts or boors, they have interpreted the gift of insight, in their characteristically forthright manner, as a sacred mission whose disavowal, on any grounds, would constitute a cowardly evasion of responsibility tantamount, in the light of the gift's divine origins, to sin. Faithful and pugnacious, they are the Eye of the Heart's crusaders, cheerfully immune to the slander and scorn their fidelity elicits. It cannot be denied, however, that in the general overview of life and things their jovial truculence, their voluntary

assumption of the role of pig-headed champion of the truth,
has been rather less effective than the sly maneuvers of the
manipulating seers, and may even have had the effect of
discrediting insights which, presented with greater diplomacy, might have been more amiably received. But diplomacy is precisely what they have renounced, and it is doubtless easy for the reader to imagine, or recall, the
imperturbable dignity with which a stubborn seer, his or her
blunt defiant analysis having been savagely interrupted as
usual, composes his or her mind amid the impatient hubbub
the simple truth aroused, and takes full force for the thou-
sandth time the exasperated outcry of a parent, spouse or
intimate friend who wheels to bellow, "Oh why don't you
keep your big mouth shut? You and your stupid remarks!"
Unless they are feeling unusually provocative or belligerent,
the stubborn seers, having made their point and kept the
faith, generally abandon the field when things reach this
pitch, saving face with a haughty silence or, even more
infuriating to those they have offended, a chuckle of hopeless contempt.

The fourth and final category of seer—after the victims of
massive deterrence, the practitioners of guile and the advo-
cates of the direct assault—are those who, in a way, combine
the experience of the previous three: somewhat of a catch-all
category, perhaps, but the reader will quickly recognize its
rather rare representatives. These seers, having drained to
the dregs life's cup of ugly surprises, cruel disappointments
and shocking revelations, have mellowed into the the placid
maturity of their disillusionment; in them the Eye of the
Heart is permanently open—we may recall the great potential liberated, upon occasion, by suffering; unfailingly kind
yet utterly detached, often of remarkably gay demeanor,
much prone to hilarity, they live in the present, allowing
their voices to utter whatever will best serve the moment
and cause the least commotion. Sometimes engagingly
insistent, but never unyielding, sometimes gently nudging,

but never calculating, most often silent, but never morose, they strive to make nothing happen themselves, but rather to move with what is already happening, a policy for which they are often criticized as arrogant. Although their respect for the Eye of the Heart, and by extension for the First Principle, may appear casual, and although some people are unable to comprehend why they respond to the truth it reveals with laughter rather than grief, these seers believe themselves to be about as serious about the world as anyone else, and their occasional astounding confessions of deadly earnestness, invariably offered with a vaguely disquieting inquisitive smile, ought not to be taken lightly. But they too, as seers, pay their price; for whether people find them cynical, refreshing, enigmatic, insensitive or effete, their apparent absence of passion coupled with a spirit of reconciliation and good will, although rarely perceived as an actual affront, is ultimately unacceptable to those to whom circumstances have bound them, and, in the fullness of time, as they know full well, this humble detachment will be the basis of a charge, almost always leveled in the form of friendly advice with a hint of admonition, as from a wiser realization, that they are being unrealistic.

The false seers, strictly speaking, bear no relationship whatsoever to the Eye of the Heart, which is, perhaps, why their counsel is so eagerly sought and so universally respected. It must be admitted, however, in all fairness to both the seekers and the seers, that this pursuit and respect are often motivated by a sort of panicky defensiveness not usually associated with people at their best, much less with the quest for enlightenment. Rapidly attaining to the somewhat precarious positions of responsibility and eminence made available in our society, the false seers seem to specialize in the canonization of self-interest and of potentially suicidal errors; their styles range from a bland, benign, almost soporific self-assurance to a staccato automatism reminiscent of robots in horror movies. They are always to be carefully distinguished, however, from the fallen seers, who, although now blind, were once blessed with vision, and through incorrigible perversity employed their gift in the pursuit of private advantage; armed with the memory of what they saw, they continue their pursuit ever more feverishly, concocting wild theories to justify the infamies to which self-hatred has driven them. The false seers, for whom the fallen seers have supreme contempt, usually admire them, and urge their consultants to emulate their zeal. The two, the false and the fallen, are often found in association, especially in bureaucracies, as if mysteriously impelled to seek each other out and in collaboration generate the atmosphere of torment and treachery in which thier personalities, and the enterprises to which such personalities gravitate, respectively fester and thrive.

The four categories of seer, of course, represent tendencies in the human spirit rather than actual individuals; always present in varying combinations, now one dominant and now another, they may be understood as the major strategies employed by the Eye of the Heart, or by the reality it unveils. But the ultimate victory of the Eye of the Heart, upon which, perhaps unfortunately, our future depends, is not the victory, no matter how cleverly accomplished or maintained, of seer over audience. The only real triumph of a divine gift, according to observers whose credentials are usually regarded as immaculate, is its acceptance within the human soul.

The sense of a separate self, precious and unique, the stalwart assumption of individual rights and prerogatives so sacrosanct that the slightest suggestion of their dispute arouses indignation, the image of oneself as a victim, beleaguered and heroic, of universal gratuitous malevolence— these are the seeds of those peculiar fanged impulses, those complacent barbarisms, casual cold-blooded calculations and stolid repudiations of good will, common sense and even sanity which challenge the tranquil and unerring vision of the Eye of the Heart. For many, of course, these "seeds" are the very foundations of reality, without which a human world, or at least the world as we live in it now, would be quite unimaginable. The inner debate, as a matter of fact, does seem to postulate the uneasy co-existence of two primordial and irreconcilable points of view, two "selves," as it were—two little birds perched upon the same branch, if the quaint image be permissible—and, as we have already noted, it is not altogether impossible that the world as it is seen through the Eye of the Heart, if not in the actual appearance of things at least in their arrangement and significance, differs markedly, even appallingly, from "the world as we live in it now," which might explain the prudence of the experienced seer, the hostility shown toward his or her proposals, and the almost invariable suppression, in the inner encounter as well as the outer, of the vision of the Eye of the Heart. But for partisans of the divine gift, and indeed of the One Who gave it, for those sufficiently courageous— or terrified or lucid or harebrained or childish or mature—to contemplate philosophies incapable of supporting "the world as we live in it now" and perhaps capable, as if to crown the insult, of supporting another, for those, in a word, who are committed, rightly or wrongly, to empathy (the inner vision), harmony (the outer vision) and truth (the total vision), the die is already cast, and "the sense of a separate self, precious and unique," however necessary to the preservation of reality as we know it, must be regarded as the principal opposition to that divine vision, impartial and ecumenical, which alone can save us from terminal disgrace. Let us then explore the inner encounter. Let us examine those challenges to the Eye of the Heart which arise within the human soul. For, despite grave doubts concerning the relevance to contemporary affairs of this inner realm, indeed concerning its very existence, it is there, we must insist, that the decisive confrontation takes place.

The Eye of the Heart, then, shares its habitation with

another entity: another claimant to judgment and discernment. This dual residence, implicit in the distressing seer-
and-audience transactions which we have analyzed fairly
thoroughly; confirmed by seemingly unmistakable evidence
of an inner debate or conflict always simmering, if not actually raging, within the human soul; confirmed yet again in
the unavoidable assumption of internal challenges to the Eye
of the Heart originating in a fiercely resentful point of view
we have provisionally referred to as the Blindness; and
summarized, both in the distinction between the Eye of the Heart
and the eyes of the head, and in the apparent co-existence of
two orders of reality corresponding to them—this dual
residency is the key, in the opinion of certain commentators,
to the entire human dilemma, indeed to the cosmic mystery
itself, and our exploration of the inner encounter, of that
confrontation we sincerely believe to be decisive, must focus
upon an identification and anatomy of the entity which,
obviously unwillingly, shares the human soul with the Eye
of the Heart. Let us call it, in deference to tradition, and in
the traditional usage, the ego.

Now the human ego, from the very outset, has strenu-
ously resisted our most resolute investigations, hidden, dissembled or falsified evidence, doctored the painstakingly
gathered data and, in a word, demonstrated powers of evasion and depths of duplicity which have, in their aggregate
effect, cast doubts upon literally every assertion ever made
regarding its true nature; its determination to remain a
mystery has been unflagging, and it would be vain to deny
that its success, at least at this point, has been complete. We
stare helplessly at an ever-expanding mass of conflicting
half-truths, each stridently defended and equally stridently
assailed in a malicious free-for-all where claims to objectivity
are so ludicrous that they, rather than the theories
advanced, are the principal target of attack. The ego, as it
were, laughs in our faces. Fortunately, however, a thorough
study is scarcely called for here, and we will confine our-

selves to those characteristics of the ego which bear directly
upon the theme of this narration, always keeping in mind a
certain inherent margin of uncertainty.

To begin with, it seems fairly safe to say that the ego is
quick to notice details invisible to the Eye of the Heart. Often
seemingly trivial or unworthy, or recalled from a remote
past with surprising vividness and heat, these details,
although ridiculously petty from an outside point of view,
are of crucial importance from the ego's perspective, especially in delicate matters, in determining the appropriate
course of action, which is usually punitive, and the hopeless
inability of the Eye of the Heart to incorporate them into its
own interpretation, invariably based upon universal compassion, is a common cause of the ego's deep skepticism
concerning the gift of vision. The ego, as a matter of fact, has
always witnessed and effortlessly committed to memory, or
inferred from frequently scanty evidence, mountains of
petty details, which it only divulges, if at all, in that mode,
peculiar to itself, called "blurting it out." Most often, however, the heterogeneous and quite considerable jumble of
odds and ends, idle gossip, vicious rumors and degenerate
metaphysics from which the ego snatches wisdom as it
inches and darts through its rather treacherous world is
shared only with very suspicious discretion, perhaps due to
the ego's characteristic, perpetual and sullen apprehension
of being misunderstood, or more specifically, of being
accused, by other egos whose motivations are by definition
suspect, of exaggeration, bias or mendacity. To a great
extent, and again characteristically, these details recorded
by the ego consist of justifications for subterfuge, vengeance or contempt, and as such are with good reason
revealed, often jokingly but through narrowed eyes as if to
test the response, only to kindred egos whose relationships
to all involved are likely to incline them toward attitudes of
sympathetic relish; in this way a sort of jovial camaraderie
blossoms, and eventually comforting groupings are con-

vened ranging in size from office cliques to entire nations. People whose egos are skilled in the gathering of promising details quickly become recognized, and invariably play a major role in the generation of those transient animosities, painful incidents and grotesque misunderstandings which form the substance of our social life and upon which our disourses focus; indeed, their skill is itself a highly significant detail immediately recorded by people similarly skilled, while those less skilled are regarded as unrealistic or naive, and even occasionally as legitimate prey in the incessant struggle for self-destructive advantages to which so many are committed. To summarize, the first inner challenge to the Eye of the Heart originates in the conflicting criteria of significance and priority by which the components of a world are selected, the criterion of the ego being, it would seem, the perpetuation and multiplication of its own kind, a fulfillment demanding single-minded concentration on the potential for strife, and that of the Eye of the Heart being the nourishing of that atmosphere of empathy and harmony in whose embrace all things flower into their truth. The ego constructs its world—which is, of course, the grim and chilling, demented and war-torn, exciting and terrifying world we all live in—from the details it quite self-righteously chooses to record, or, when necessary, to invent, fearing, perhaps with good reason, that in a world constructed by the Eye of the Heart it would lose that thrilling sense of encirclement by mortal enemies, that sense of constant threat and imminent crushing triumph, which is the very rationale for its existence. Such a loss of rationale, indeed, as the Eye of the Heart actually suffers—to the indulgent satisfaction of the ego's defenders, whose great pride is their liberation from illusion—in the reassuring depravity of the ego's world.

From the watchful perpspective of the ego the insights of the Eye of the Heart often present themselves as sudden impulses, born of weakness or inexplicable perversity. How often are people with strong egos compelled to stifle ruthlessly, in the name of prudence, self-restraint or mature wisdom, those impulses to kindness, forgiveness, generosity, self-sacrifice and the like which arise without warning from some phantom "other self" evidently isolated in a private dream world! For the ego is no less aware than the Eye of the Heart that another presence shares, and indeed contests dominion within, the human recepticle with which it so fervently identifies. Continually as impulses, continuously as a vague gnawing doubt, a sense that something, perhaps the whole scheme of things, is gravely amiss, the insights and subversive insistence of the Eye of the Heart disrupt with wild inclinations the ego's otherwise keen, almost military concentration and inhibit with somber misgivings amounting at times to fatalism the otherwise alert maneuvers with which it competes for survival. The ego also is aware of an internal challenge, of strange impulses to seek a reconciliation rather than a rout, to mollify rather than subjugate, to embrace rather than assault, to smile rather than sneer, to listen rather than refute, to heal rather than kill, to love rather than hate, and, as the Eye of the Heart, equating itself with vision, can only conceive its opposition as a form of blindness, so the ego, equating itself with reason, can only conceive its opposition as a form of madness. The latter indictment, we must with sorrow admit, is all to often substantiated by the horrendous experience of socialization in modern society—an experience which, if I may be permitted the irony, is often described, like so many others, as "eye-opening."

On the other hand, and paradoxically enough, the ego itself is notoriously impulsive, notoriously passionate, and when in heat, as it were, is prone to perceive the insights of the Eye of the Heart as mere moral imperatives, mere philosophy, mere objective truth—as if the gift of the First Principle took no account of those sudden spiritual opportunities whose prompt seizure and vigorous exploitation is a measure of our vitality, nor of the necessity to obey impulses on pain of collapsing into mere contemplativeness. In this classic phase of the inner debate, the ego, which almost invariably emerges victorious, is pestered by annoying memories of those tedious abstractions and time-tested principles, perhaps intrinsic to the cosmic economy, which the human race, despite nearly superhuman efforts, has never been able to quash completely; these vexing reminders, usually interpreted as misguided "second thoughts" stemming from timidity, or as temptations to stagnation originating in the fear of disillusion, are resisted by the ego not on rational grounds—which would be to concede significance where there is none—but as a point of honor, and in the solemn awareness that succumbing to their cloying restraint would lay it open to the charge, perhaps more feared than any other of the ego's innumerable fears, of being insufficiently aggressive.

Aggressiveness, as a matter of fact, is the ego's principal means of grasping reality—along with rage, lust, greed and concupiscence in general—and its absence in the approach of the Eye of the Heart, in the insidious impulses and bothersome reminders referred to above, is undoubtedly the true basis of the ego's firm rejection of divine vision, as its detection of cowardice, impudence or wishy-washy subterfuge lurking in that absence explains the shrewd leer or bitter scowl with which it often greets those promptings to self-effacement and friendly respect whose complete suppression, although clearly within our reach, has proven so difficult to achieve. Indeed, it would not be going too far to say that aggressiveness, with all its thrills and terrors, its creativity and destructiveness, is the ego's only assurance that it exists and that the world is real, or at least comprehensible. The ego's implacable opposition to the Eye of the Heart, seen in this light, is neither an accident stemming from dual residency nor a satanic caprice, but quite obviously a necessary struggle to protect and perpetuate that doomed world, the fruit of its own suicidal ardor, in which it alone can survive.

The only other passion in the ego that might compete for supremacy with aggressiveness is fear—fear of the world, fear of truth, fear of life, fear of death and, most harrowing of all, fear of other egos. The Eye of the Heart, of course, being devoid of desire and loving only the truth—which it more or less identifies with the point of view of the First Principle—is a stranger to fear, and it is principally their fearlessness, their total indifference to public opinion, their unconditional compassion, that make its insights seem so laughably unrealistic to the ego. For the ego is always deeply and absorbingly entangled with other egos in a web of jealous intrigue and interwoven battle plans where the slightest misstep can be fatal, and fear, as it were, is the very light that illuminates the strands, without which the web would be invisible and even, in a sense, non-existent; fearlessness, or simple honesty, in such a context, would quite literally amount to mindlessness, and its expression, if taken seriously, could only be interpreted as yet another cunning ploy, introduced perhaps for a temporary startling effect to serve as a smoke screen for clandestine maneuvers. In a word, without fear the individual ego would be doomed, and were the loss of fear to become by some catastrophe epidemic the entire world of egos—which is, as we have indicated, this very world in which we are at present both imprisoned and enthroned—would simply vanish into thin air: the death which the ego fears, paradoxically enough, is the death of fear. But here we approach, once again, the dizzy heights of metaphysics, whose negotiation, as we remarked before, is best left to experts. Suffice it to say that the necessity of fear, as of aggressiveness, so fundamental to the argument of the ego, is another sore point in the inner encounter, whose exploration we have nearly completed, in which the insights of divine vision are so often casually or viciously stifled before they can face that communal disinterest, derision and animosity deplored in the first half of this narration.

The ego, then, is none other than that "separate self, precious and unique" but for whose self-centeredness, as it were, the Eye of the Heart would be free to fulfill unhampered the merciful intention of the First Principle. And sad to say, the probability of the ego's surrender to an approach clearly more promising than its own, at least in terms of humanity's survival, or to any other approach whatsoever, is, we are compelled to admit, rather slight; the ego's readily offended sense of its importance and centrality, its inherent and perpetual terror of extinction, its angry certainty that it is always in the right, and its indestructible conviction that without its feverish contribution, indeed without its presence merely as a spectator, the world would immediately collapse—these traits alone, not to mention the insatiable appetites which are its pride, are a sufficient guarantee of its grim determination to remain with us, as the very self within each of us, until the end. The Eye of the Heart's conflict with the ego is to the death.

But if our situation is not reassuring, neither is it hopeless. It has been argued that, as the curtain descends, more and more people are seeing with the Eye of the Heart, and if the truth they see is hideous, it is nonetheless the truth, and truth alone, as we have been repeatedly informed, can save us from ourselves. In deteriorating circumstances the Eye of the Heart acquires a certain precarious advantage; indeed, it was precisely for recourse in deteriorating circumstances, whose inevitable advent was accurately foreseen by the First Principle, that the divine gift was given.

The question is often raised as to the relationship, if any, between the Eye of the Heart and that love which, according to some observers, "moves the sun and the other stars." In the light of the foregoing, it would seem obvious that such a relationship does indeed exist, and that it is at least as intimate as other more celebrated relationships in our society. It may even be that the two, the Eye of the Heart and the love that sustains the universe, are in reality one and the same, an intimacy which suggests that, at least in the moment of exaltation, the seer may with justification claim to be at one with the immense inscrutable cosmic purpose in which we are safely contained: in tune with things, as it were: in touch with reality. This being so, it follows with inescapable rigor that all opposition to the Eye of the Heart is not only impetuous but clearly, in the long run, doomed. And if there are some who in their restless fervor nod impatiently, or in their seasoned valor smile sarcastically, and demand a reassurance more contemporary, more mechanical, more rooted in the historical sciences, yet there are others who find in this ultimate vindication not only solace but a peace which apparently, and perhaps appropriately, surpasses understanding.

Epilog

by John Street

Some three months after the "Perspectives on the Crisis of Contemporary Life" Conference concluded I had occasion to be returning to San Francisco from an assignment in San Diego, and on an impulse took the Sandstone exit, thinking to wander a bit about the grounds of the College of the West and perhaps, by reawakening the memories of my sojourn there, discover, or indeed create, new depths in the experience—a strategy I have employed from time to time in the past with unpredictable success.

It was a Sunday, late afternoon; the campus was fairly deserted. I strolled through the long shadows over to the Adam Bell Center, in whose modern auditorium, now empty and silent, the papers had been delivered. I took a seat in the last row and allowed the ghosts to enter, each inseparable in my mind from a "perspective" on the contemporary world and, which amounted to the same thing for me now, on my life. I believe it was gratitude, a gratitude that had required time to mature, more than a simple wish to extend the experience, that motivated my impulse on the freeway.

There was Walter Frank striding to the podium, settling his papers with confident anticipation and looking up with a bright smile of welcome; Mark Harrison, hawk-like and stiffly erect, his eyes darting from face to face in the audience; Sister Angela Maria Prescott, bent and frail in her black habit, being helped up the steps by Dr. Harrison, who had hurried to her side when she paused at the edge of the stage—a letter informing me of her death was awaiting me on my desk in San Francisco; Pierre Flynn, spruce, overly courteous and inscrutable, chuckling over the hopeless, and fatal, intransigence of human nature; Amy Rosenblatt, her

voice ringing and passionate, summoning us to our evolutionary destiny; and Louis di Prima, speaking slowly and
clearly, without once smiling, notifying us of the end of the
world.

Seated in the cool silence, I recalled that what had struck
me most forcefully on my return from the Conference was
the unchanged world—the same headlines, brutal and prophetic, the same sputtering drift toward an ultimate violence, the same fleeting desperations and fragile compensa-
tions, the same defiant charges into the same implacable
emptiness—almost, I smiled to myself, as if I had uncon-
sciously assumed at Sandstone, and then been shocked to
discover I was mistaken, that the whole human race, by
some miracle granted in concession to an overwhelming
appropriateness, was also hearing the presentations at the
Conference, perhaps in dreams, and would be undertaking,
even before I returned, the immense labor of rectification.
My shock, however, was due not to a disappointed fantasy
but rather to the education of my vision; the world was the
same, only I was seeing it now with a greater, almost a
rueful, clarity. The papers, on their various levels, had been
on the mark: they had cast light.

But would they, I thought to myself, make any difference?
A pointless question. We learn, as our strength of mind
develops, to execute our tasks in the assumption that they
have meaning—and perhaps thereby give them the only true
meaning they will ever have—and in this particular instance
that meaning would be compromised not a whit should the
human race choose to pursue its suicidal career, which
seemed quite likely, as if there had never been a Conference
at Sandstone. The Hardwood Fund, out of concern and in its
generosity, had sponsored a Conference on the Crisis of
Contemporary Life: the papers had been duly solicited and
delivered: I was engaged to edit them. My task was to cast
their wisdom and warning into the world, in the present
volume, and in so doing to pass on what I had received as

those six people to whom I was indebted had passed on what
they had received: I could do no more, and no less. If my
experience at the Conference was more than professional,
in that it had a private significance, my responsibility was
not. My task, in the final analysis, was quite impersonal.

The darkness which had fallen upon the auditorium
summoned me from my reverie. It was time to leave. I rose
to my feet and stood for a moment, listening to the silence as
three months earlier I had listened to voices. I am not a
metaphysician nor, as I mentioned in my journal, a senti-
mentalist. I have been a practical, rather unimaginative man,
competent in my discipline, reliable in my rather small circle
of acquaintance, patient with human imperfection, my own
and other's. Such have been my chosen virtues, and such
their scale. I sought, however, in that moment, to plumb the
depths of my soul, and from those depths to acknowledge
my gratitude to those to whom I owed so much, and to
express my humility, for I can offer no concrete tribute in
this realm, before the knowledge they worshiped and the
truth they loved. I bowed my head.

BIBLIOGRAPHY

Adam, Karl. *The Spirit of Catholicism.* Doubleday: 1954.

Agee, James & Evans, Walker. *Let Us Now Praise Famous Men.* Ballantine: 1966

Alexander, Hartley Burr. *The World's Rim.* University of Nebraska Press: 1953. An excellent study of Native American life.

Alvarez, A. *The Savage God.* Random House: 1972.

Amnesty International. *Report on Torture.* Farrar, Straus & Giroux: 1973.

Aquinas, Thomas. *An Aquinas Reader.* Doubleday: 1972.

Arberry, A.J. (translator). *The Doctrine of the Sufis.* Cambridge University Press: 1977.

Augustine. *On Christian Doctrine.* Bobbs-Merrill: 1958.
   The City of God. Doubleday 1958.

Aurobindo. *Essays on the Gita.* Sri Aurobindo Ashram Trust: 1972. In my opinion, his best book. Here his own vision is bound to Scripture; elsewhere he tends to leave us behind.
   The Life Divine (2 volumes). Sri Aurobindo Ashram Trust: 1973.
   The Synthesis of Yoga. Sri Aurobindo Ashram Trust: 1973.

Baran, Paul. *The Political Economy of Growth.* Monthly Review: 1962.

Baran, Paul & Sweezy, Paul. *Monopoly Capital.* Monthly Review: 1966. A little dated, but about the best we can hope for from the Marxian approach.

Barnett, John (editor). *Our Mistreated World.* Dow Jones Books: 1966.

Bates, Marston. *The Forest and the Sea.* Vintage: 1960.

Benedict, Ruth. *Pattern of Culture.* Houghton, Mifflin: 1959.

Bergman, Arlene Eisen. *Women of Vietnam.* People's Press: 1974.

Bergson, Henri. *The Two Sources of Morality and Religion.* Doubleday: 1954. A classic. Don't be put off by the 20-page paragraphs and the absence of sub-headings.

Bierhost, John (editor). *In the Trail of the Wind.* Farrar, Straus & Giroux: 1971. Native American poetry, chants and oration. The fading echo of pre-civilized harmony.

Black Elk. *The Sacred Pipe* Penguin: 1971. A great book. Excellent footnotes by Joseph Epes Brown.
   Black Elk Speaks. University of Nebraska Press: 1961.

Bonhoeffer, Dietrich. *Creation and Fall, Temptation.* MacMillan: 1971. A bit grim.

Bookchin, Murray. *Post-Scarcity Anarchism.* Ramparts: 1971. The best anarchist we have. His books are filled with fine insights and sound scholarship.
Our Synthetic Environment. Harper & Row: 1974

Boyer & Morais. *Labor's Untold Story.* United Electrical, Radio and Machine Workers of America (UE): 1975.

Branfman, Fred (compiler). *Voice from the Plain of Jars.* Harper & Row: 1972.

Brantl, George (editor). *Catholicism.* Braziller: 1962. Well done.

Braverman, Harry. *Labor and Monopoly Capitalism.* Monthly Review: 1974. A classic of the Marxist approach. Indispensable for an understanding of the modern labor process.

Brecher, Jeremy. *Strike!* Fawcett: 1974. Populist, radical, anti-union.

Buber, Martin. *I and Thou.* Scribner's: 1970.
Between Man and Man. Beacon: 1955.

Campbell, Joseph. *The Hero With A Thousand Faces.* Princeton University Press: 1949. Absorbing, like all his books, but, again like all his books, a trifle too sweeping.
The Masks of God: Occidental Mythology. Penguin: 1976.
The Masks of God: Oriental Mythology. Viking: 1962.
Myths to Live By. Bantam: 1973.

Carson, Rachel. *Silent Spring.* Houghton Mifflin: 1962.

Casagrande, Joseph M. (editor). *In The Company Of Man.* Harper: 1960.

Cassirer, Ernst. *An Essay On Man.* Yale University Press: 1944.

Chuang Tzu (edited by Thomas Merton). *The Way of Chuang Tzu.* New Directions: 1965. Good introduction by Merton.

College of Natural Resources, University of California at Berkeley.
Environmental Studies, IDS 10. Fall Quarter: 1976.
Global Problems, IDS 10B. Winter Quarter: 1976.
Global Environmental Problems, IDS 10B. Winter Quarter: 1977.

Commoner, Barry. *The Closing Circle.* Bantam: 1972. An ecology classic.

Conze, Edward. *Buddhism: Its Essence and Development.* Harper & Row: 1975. A fine introduction. I recommend his memoirs. You'll see why when you read them!
Buddhist Thought in India. University of Michigan Press: 1977.

Conze, Edward, et al. (editors). *Buddhist Texts Through The Ages.* Harper & Row: 1964.

Coomaraswamy, Ananda K. *Buddha and the Gospel of Buddhism.* Harper & Row: 1964. A fine book.
The Bugbear of Literacy. Perennial: 1979.
Hinduism and Buddhism. Philosophical Library: no date given.

Cotlow, Louis. *The Twilight of the Primitive.* Ballantine: 1973.

Council on Interracial Books for Children. *Chronicles of American Indian Protest.* Fawcett: 1971.

Cronyn, George W. (editor). *American Indian Poetry.* Liveright: 1934.

David-Neel, Alexandra. *Buddhism: Its Doctrines and Its Methods.* Avon: 1979. An excellent basic introduction.

Dawson, Christopher. *Progress and Religion.* Doubleday: 1969.

Day, A. Grove (editor). *The Sky Clears.* University of Nebraska Press: 1951.

Deloria, Vine. *God is Red.* Dell: 1973.

Des Pres, Terrence. *The Survivor.* Oxford University Press: 1976. A memorable book.

De Wulf, Maurice. *The System of Thomas Aquinas.* Dover: 1959.

Dorst, Jean. *Before Nature Dies.* Houghton Mifflin: 1970.

Dubos, Rene. *Mirage of Health.* Harper & Row: 1971.
So Human An Animal. Scribner's: 1968

Eakins, David et al. *Socialist Revolution.* Vol. I, No. 1 Jan-Feb 1970, Vol, I, No. 2 March-April 1970.

Eaton, John. *Political Economy.* International: 1966. Superior to the Leontiev book of the same title.

Eckhart. *Meister Eckhart.* Harper & Row: 1941.

Eiseley, Loren. *The Immense Journey.* Random House: 1946.

Eliade, Mircea. *Myths, Dreams, and Mysteries.* Harper & Row: 1967. A great Master. Everything he wrote is precious.
The Sacred and the Profane. Harcourt, Brace & World: 1959.
The Quest. University of Chicago Press: 1969.
Patterns in Comparative Religion. World: 1963.
Rites and Symbols of Initiation. Harper & Row: 1958.

Myth and Reality. Harper & Row: 1963.
The Two and the One. University of Chicago Press: 1965.
Shamanism. Princeton University Press: 1972.
Yoga: Immortality and Freedom. Princeton University Press: 1970.
The Myth of the Eternal Return, or, Cosmos and History. Princeton University Press: 1971.
Edited by Eliade:
Gods, Goddesses and Myths of Creation. Harper & Row: 1967.
Man and the Sacred. Harper & Row: 1967.
Death, Afterlife and Eschatology. Harper & Row: 1967.
From Medicine Men to Muhammed. Harper & Row: 1967.
(Parts 1, 2, 3 and 4 of *From Primitives to Zen.*)

Ellul, Jacques. *The Technological Society.* Random House: 1964. Classic autopsy of the West.

Emerson, Ralph Waldo. *Selected Writings.* Random House: 1940.

Fanon, Frantz. *Studies in a Dying Colonialism.* Monthly Review: 1965.

Federal Writers' Project. *These Are Our Lives.* Norton: 1975.

Feuer, Lewis. *Ideology and the Ideologists.* Harper: 1975.

Frank, Andre Gunder. *Capitalism and Underdevelopment in Latin America.* Monthly Review: 1957.

Frank, Waldo. *The Rediscovery of Man.* Braziller: 1958. Many fine insights, but a bit impetuous.

Freeman, Jo (editor). *Women: A Feminist Perspective.* Mayfield: 1979.

Gibb, H.A.R. *Mohammedanism.* Oxford University Press: 1962.

Giedion, Siegfried. *Mechanisation Takes Command.* Norton: 1969. Marvellously interesting, filled with profound perceptions. Excellent photographs and illustrations.

Gilson, Etienne. *God and Philosophy.* Yale University Press: 1941

Glenn, Michael (editor). *Voices from the Asylum.* Harper & Row: 1974.

Goffman, Erving. *Asylums.* Doubleday: 1961.

Goldschmidt, Walter (editor). *Exploring the Ways of Mankind.* (Second edition) Holt, Rinehart & Winston: 1960.

Gorz, Andre. *Strategy for Labor.* Beacon: 1968.

Guenon, Rene. *Symbolism of the Cross.* Luzac: 1975.
The Reign of Quantity and The Signs of the Times. Penguin: 1972. A seminal work of the traditionalist group. Indispensable.

Guevara. *Che Guevara Speaks.* Merit: 1967.

Gutman, Hervert G. *Work, Culture and Society in Industrializing America.* Knopf: 1976.

Hammond, Peter B. (editor). *Cultural and Social Anthropology.* MacMillan: 1964.
Cultural and Social Anthropology (Second edition). Macmillan: 1975.

Handlin, Oscar. *The Uprooted.* Little, Brown: 1971. A great book.

Hersey, John. *Hiroshima.* Bantam: 1948.

Herskovitz, Melville. *Economic Athropology.* Norton: 1965.
Cultural Anthropology. Knopf: 1955.

Heschel, Abraham Joshua. *God In Search Of Man: A Philosophy Of Judaism.* Farrar, Straus & Giroux: 1955.

Hinton, William. *Fanshen.* Random House: 1968.

Isherwood, Christopher (editor). *Vedanta for the Western World.* Vedanta Press: 1945.
Vedanta for Modern Man. New American Library: 1972.

Jaeger, Werner. *Paideia.* (Three volumes) Oxford University Press: Volume I, 1939; Volume II, 1943; Volume III, 1944. Classic. The section on Socrates is superb.
Humanism and Theology. Marquette University Press: 1980.
Early Christianity and Greek Paideia. Oxford University Press: 1977.

James, William. *The Varieties of Religious Experience.* New American Library: 1958.

Kahler, Erich. *Man The Measure.* Braziller: 1961. A fine overview of western civilization.

Kahn, Kathy (editor). *Hillbilly Women.* Avon: 1974.

Kapleau, Philip. *The Three Pillars of Zen.* Doubleday: 1980.

Katz, Jane B. (editor). *I Am The Fire Of Time.* E.P. Dutton: 1977.

Kedward, Roderick. *The Anarchists.* American Heritage Press: 1971. Lively text, wonderful photographs.

Keller, Helen. *The Story of My Life.* Dell: 1974.

Khan, Hazrat Inayat. *The Unity of Religious Ideals.* Sufi Order Publications: 1979.

Kracauer, Siegfried. *From Caligari to Hitler.* Princeton University Press: 1947.

Leontiev, A. *Political Economy.* Proletarian Publishers: no date given. Inferior to the Eaton book of the same title.

Leopold, Aldo. *A Sand County Almanac.* Oxford University Press: 1966.

Lester, Julius. *To Be A Slave.* Dell: 1968

Lings, Martin. *Ancient Beliefs and Modern Superstitions.* Unwin: 1980. A fine basic text of the traditionalist group.
   A Sufi Saint of the Twentieth Century. University of California Press: 1973.
   What is Sufism? University of California Press: 1977. Excellent.

Lukacs, Georg. *History and Class Consciousness.* MIT Press: 1971. Dense.

Macciocchi, Maria Antonietta. *Daily Life in Revolutionary China.* Monthly Review: 1972.

Marcuse, Herbert. *One-Dimensional Man.* Beacon: 1964.
   Counter-Revolution and Revolt. Beacon: 1972.

Maritain, Jacques. *Existence and The Existent.* Doubleday: 1956.

Marx, Karl *Capital: A Critical Analysis of Capitalist Production.* (Volume I) International: 1947. There's no substitute.
   Capital: The Process of Circulation of Capital. (Volume II) Progress: 1967.
   Capital: The Process of Capitalist Production as a Whole. (Volume III) Progress: 1966.
   Grundrisse. Vintage: 1973. Along with *Capital I,* this is the Master's contribution.
   Manifesto of the Communist Party. Foreign Languages Press, Peking: 1968.

Matthiessen, Peter. *Wildlife in America.* Viking: 1964.

Matthiessen, Peter and Porter, Eliot. *The Tree Where Man Was Born/ The African Experience.* Avon: 1974.

McIntyre, Joan (editor). *Wind in the Waters.* Scribner's: 1974.

McLuhan, T.C. (compiler). *Touch The Earth.* Pocket Books: 1972.

Meltzer, Milton. *Bread and Roses.* Random House: 1967.
   Brother, can you spare a dime? Random House: 1969. Both books are excellent blends of history and oral history.

Merton, Thomas. *The Ascent to Truth.* Harcourt Brace Jovanovich: 1981. A fine study of the Christian contemplative life.

Mooney, James. *The Ghost-Dance Religion and Wounded Knee.* Dover: 1973. A great book.

Morais & Cahn. *Gene Debs.* International: 1948.

Morgan, George W. *The Meaning of Man.* Doubleday: 1961. Brilliant, beautiful book by a Catholic scholar.

Mowat, Farley. *People of the Deer.* Little, Brown: 1952.
A Whale for the Killing. Penguin: 1973.

Mumford, Lewis. *The Transformations of Man.* Collier Books: 1956. A great Master, a great humanist. His contribution beggars praise.
The Condition of Man. Harcourt Brace Jovanovich: 1944.
The Conduct of Life. Harcourt Brace Jovanovich: 1951.
Technics and Civilization. Harcourt Brace & World: 1951.
The City in History. Harcourt, Brace & World: 1934.
Technics and Human Development (The Myth of the Machine, Volume I) Harcourt Brace Jovanovich: 1967.
The Pentagon of Power (The Myth of the Machine, Volume II) Harcourt Brace Jovanovich: 1970.

Nasr, Seyyed Hossein. *Man and Nature.* Unwin: 1976. Passionate and incisive book by a leading traditionalist.
Sufi Essays. State University of New York Press: 1973.

Needleman, Jacob (editor). *The Sword of Gnosis.* Penguin: 1974. We are indebted to Needleman for introducing the traditionalists. Almost shocking at first—challenging Darwin!—but then it all falls into place. A fine collection of essays.

Origen. *An Exhortation to Martyrdom, Prayer and Selected Works.* Paulist Press: 1979.

Ortega y Gasset, Jose. *An Interpretation of Universal History.* Norton: 1973. A shameful book.

Otto, Rudolph. *The Idea of the Holy.* Oxford University Press: 1923. A classic.
Mysticism East and West. MacMillan: 1970.

Packard, Vance. *A Nation of Strangers.* David McKay: 1972.

Prabhavananda. *The Spiritual Heritage of India.* Vedanta Press: 1979. The best introduction I know of.

Prem (Sri Krishna). *The Yoga of the Bhagavat Gita.* Penguin: 1973. A fine study by a Western-born master, Ronald Henry Nixon.

Price, Richard (editor). *Maroon Societies.* Doubleday: 1973.

Radhakrishnan, Sarvepalli. *Selected Writings on Philosophy, Religion and Culture* (edited by Robert A. McDermott). Dutton: 1970.
The Bhagavadgita. Harper & Row: 1973.
The Hindu View of Life. Allen and Unwin: 1927.
Eastern Religions and Western Thought. Oxford University Press: 1939.

Rubin, Lillian Breslow. *Worlds of Pain.* Basic Books: 1976.

Schimmel, Annamarie. *Mystical Dimensions of Islam.* University of North Carolina Press: 1975.

Scholem, Gershom. *Major Trends in Jewish Mysticism.* Schocken: 1961.
On the Kabbalah and its Symbolism. Schocken: 1965.

Schuon, Frithjof. *Stations of Wisdom.* Perennial: 1961. Schuon's work is informed by grace. He is the greatest writer on comparative religion who ever lived.
Gnosis, Divine Wisdom. Perennial: 1959.
Esoterism as Principle and as Way. Perennial: 1981.
Islam and the Perennial Philosophy. World of Islam Festival Publishing Company: 1976.
Light on the Ancient Worlds. Perennial: 1965.
Understanding Islam. Unwin: 1976.

Schwartz, Barry & Disch, Robert (editors). *White Racism.* Dell: 1970.

Seidenberg, Roderick. *Post-Historic Man.* Viking: 1974. Another classic autopsy.

Seton, Ernest Thompson (compiler). *The Gospel of the Red Man.* Seton Village: 1963.

Shankara. *The Crest-Jewel of Discrimination.* Vedanta Press: 1947.

Sharafuddin. *The Hundred Letters.* Paulist Press: 1980. A great book by a Sufi Master.

Shepard, Paul & McKinley, Daniel (editors). *The Subversive Science.* Houghton Mifflin: 1969. Excellent ecology essays.

Shorris, Earl. *The Death of the Great Spirit.* New American Library: 1971. A grim and serious book.

Simpson, George Gaylord. *The Meaning of Evolution.* Yale University Press: 1949. Solid science.

Steiner, Stan. *The New Indians.* Dell: 1968.

Storer, John H. *The Web of Life.* New American Library: 1953.

Suzuki, D.T. *Essays in Zen Buddhism.* First Series, Grove: 1961; Second Series, Samuel Weiser: 1971; Third Series, Samuel Weiser: 1971.
Zen and Japanese Culture. Princeton University Press: 1970.
Zen Buddhism. Doubleday: 1956.
The Awakening of Zen. Prajna Press: 1980.
Studies in Zen. Dell: 1955.

Sweezy, Paul. *The Theory of Capitalist Development.* Monthly Review: 1942. The best commentary if you simply can't face *Capital.*
The Present as History. Monthly Review: 1953.

Sweezy, Paul & Magdoff, Harry. *The Dynamics of U.S. Capitalism.* Monthly Review: 1972.

Tagore, Rabindranath. *The Religion of Man.* Beacon Press: 1961.

Terkel, Studs. *Working.* Avon: 1972.
Division Street America. Random House: 1967.

Thompson, E.P. *The Making of the English Working Class.* Vintage: 1963.

Tillich, Paul. *Dynamics of Faith.* Harper & Row: 1958.
The Shaking of the Foundations. Scribner's: 1963
The Eternal Now. Scribner's: 1963.
The New Being. Scribner's: 1955.
Systematic Theology. University of Chicago Press: Volume I, 1951; Volume II, 1957; Volume III, 1963. I liked Volume II, "Existence and the Christ," the best. Not for casual reading.

Toynbee, Arnold. *A Study of History.* Volumes IV, V and VI. Oxford University Press.
A Study of History. Abridgement by D.C. Somervell, 2 volumes. Oxford University Press.

Underhill, Evelyn. *Mysticism.* Dutton: 1961.

Underhill, Ruth Murray. *Singing for Power.* Ballantine: 1973.

Vann, Gerald. *The Heart of Man.* Doubleday: 1960.

Villasenor, David. *Tapestries in Sand.* Naturegraph: 1963.

Vivekananda. *Jnana-Yoga.* Vedanta Press: 1973.
Bhakti-Yoga. Vedanta Press: 1974.
Karma-Yoga. Vedanta Press: 1974.

Watts, Alan. *The Way of Zen.* New American Library: 1959. A good introduction.
Tao:The Watercourse Way. Pantheon: 1975.

Weaver, Thomas (editor). *To See Ourselves.* Scott, Foresman: 1973.

Weber, Max. *The Protestant Ethic and the Spirit of Capitalism.* Scribner's: 1958.

Weisberg, Barry. *Ecocide in Indochina.* Harper & Row: 1970.

Whitman, Walt. *Complete Poetry and Selected Prose.* Houghton Mifflin: 1959.

Williams, John Alden (editor). *Islam.* Pocket Books: 1963.

www.ingramcontent.com/pod-product-compliance
Lightning Source LLC
Chambersburg PA
CBHW021057090426
42738CB00006B/381